SKIING WITH
THE WHOLE BODY

SKIING WITH THE WHOLE BODY

Jack Heggie

North Atlantic Books
Berkeley, California

Also by the same author:
RUNNING WITH THE WHOLE BODY

Published by:
North Atlantic Books
P.O. Box 12327
Berkeley, California 94712

Cover photograph by Jerry Sinkovec
Photography: Moses Street, Boulder, Colorado
Ski clothing courtesy Spyder Active Sports, Boulder, Colorado
Cover and book design by Paula Morrison

ISBN 1-55643-140-6

These exercises have been tested and found to work for people in good health. If you have any questions about your fitness and your ability to do the exercises, consult your physician before starting the program.

The Feldenkrais Method, Functional Integration, and Awareness Through Movement are registered trademarks of the Feldenkrais Guild.

SKIING WITH THE WHOLE BODY is sponsored by the Society for the Study of Native Arts and Sciences, a nonprofit educational corporation whose goals are to develop an educational and crosscultural perspective linking various scientific, social, and artistic fields; to nurture a holistic view of arts, sciences, humanities, and healing; and to publish and distribute literature on the relationship of mind, body, and nature.

2   3   4   5   6   7   8   9   /   01   00   99   98   97

For
Marty, Chris, and John —
and all the good days.

Acknowledgements

This book evolved from my studies with Moshe Feldenkrais, D. Sc. Without his pioneering research in the practical functioning of the human motor system, the book would not exist. The awareness lessons for improving skiing ability are a direct adaptation of the ideas and methods that he presented in his Awareness Through Movement® lessons.

Karl Pribram, M.D., Ph.D., contributed original ideas through his book *Languages of the Brain* which lead to the concept of the Moving Mind.

I acknowledge here also my students, who put up with my unorthodox ideas and allowed me to use their bodies as my experimental laboratory while I developed the method over a period of many years.

And finally, Ian Jackson, who suggested the final form of the book, and engendered the umpteenth, and final, rewrite.

Table of Contents

"You cannot teach a man anything. You can only help him to discover it within himself."

—Galileo Galilei

The Spirit of Skiing

There is a spirit that abides deep in the heart of the mountains. It is the spirit of skiing.

On cold winter days she comes forth from her lair and searches for those worthy of her favor.

Through the high mountain valleys and over the jagged peaks she flies.

If you would seek the spirit of skiing, you must prepare yourself well.

On each day, you must go up and test yourself against the mountain.

And little by little, day by day, you will find your way.

As you take the measure of the steeper trails and the bigger bumps, you will come closer and closer.

If you are touched by the spirit of skiing, you will know the joy of the mountains, and the freedom of the wind.

If you become one with the spirit of skiing, you will have the power of the mountains, and of the wind, and of other things for which there are no words.

And when the spirit comes, you may know her by these signs. First, by her beauty, which surpasses all others. And second, by her movements, which are like nothing on this earth.

The spirit is willing. She awaits you patiently in her high mountain fastness.

Seek her and she will be yours.

Introduction

If someone had told me just a few years ago that I would soon write a downhill ski instruction book, I would have laughed in his face, and with good reason. At the age of 32, after about 14 years of skiing, I was a "permanent intermediate" skier.

I had begun skiing when I went to college in Colorado, and when I graduated four years later, I could call myself a solid intermediate-level skier.

But then, for the next ten years, I couldn't seem to improve at all. I tried lessons, books, and skiing with better skiers, but nothing seemed to work. I was stuck. Gradually, I began to get the idea that high-level skiing required something I didn't have. And what that "something" might be seemed the ultimate mystery, at least to me.

And so one day, late in the afternoon, near the end of the ski season, standing at the top of a run, after what seemed like the ten thousandth day of trying to improve and not getting any results, I had about decided I had had enough of skiing. I was sick and tired of being stuck at a low level of ability, and not being able to improve. I was ready to quit.

What I didn't know, standing there, was that in just a few seconds I would have an experience so profound that it would forever alter the course of my life, and launch me on a path that would keep me on skis till the end of my days.

Just a few hours earlier, I had a peculiar idea. For the past several years I had been studying an awareness system that seemed to hold a promise of improved movement and therefore, I hoped, of improved skiing. I had spent quite a few hours rolling around on the floor trying to improve my "awareness," and although I felt I was learning something, my skiing ability remained unchanged.

However, that morning I had the idea of using the awareness approach directly on skis, something I had never tried before. I had spent an hour or so skiing very slowly back and forth across the trail, and leaning forward and back, and left and right, and trying to discover just what I did with the various parts of my body as I moved. I made a number of interesting discoveries, but when I went back to skiing, there was still no improvement.

And so I turned my tips down the hill, and began to ski. I was on a designated intermediate trail, but it was on the easy side for such, and I wasn't having too much trouble staying under control. I was moving with my usual stiff, ungainly style, like the majority of skiers on the hill.

But suddenly, I felt a strange muscular shift somewhere deep in my gut. It was a most peculiar feeling. Something deep down inside of my innermost being seemed to reposition itself. I started to frame the question "What was that?" but suddenly my world exploded. I felt my knees bend and my back straighten, seemingly of their own accord, and my skis began to whip left and right in what felt like perfect linked parallel turns. My hands were moving to make exact pole plants, and I was flying down the mountain with the skill and grace that I had always dreamed of. This, I knew without a doubt, is *skiing*.

The trees were streaking past me in a blur, and I felt my body working like a smooth, powerful machine. I had the strange, paradoxical feeling that I was totally out of control, and yet that I was skiing perfectly.

And then, suddenly, a strange thought raced through my head: "You can't do this." I looked down at my feet and froze up and fell, losing my skis and goggles.

I shook off the snow, quickly replaced my equipment, and immediately started back down the hill. I wanted to ski like that again!

But inexplicably, I was again skiing as I always did. In comparison to my "breakthrough," my usual way of skiing now felt especially heavy and dull. It was nearing four o'clock, and I only had time for one more run. I tried to recreate the magic feeling of perfect motion that I had earlier, but it was gone.

The following day was the last of the season for me, and even though I repeated the awareness exercises I thought had triggered my breakthrough, my skiing remained unchanged.

So I returned to my field engineering job at sea, and spent the next ten months in the middle of the Atlantic Ocean brooding over my experience. As I turned it over and over in my mind, it began to assume an air of unreality, and at times I thought that my breakthrough must have been a dream. That kind of skiing seemed so foreign to my usual ways of moving.

I had always thought of myself as one of the most uncoordinated people on the face of the earth. In school, I was always the last to be picked when choosing sides for any kind of game. If I chased a fly ball, I was always ten feet away when it hit the ground. If I ran any distance, my throat would start to burn and I would have to stop. No sport—and I tried a lot of them—seemed to work for me, and skiing hadn't been much different. I used to joke to myself—but it was a bitter joke—that anyone less coordinated than me would be in a wheelchair.

But as I thought more and more about what had happened to me, I came to one indisputable conclusion. If I had skied perfectly for those few seconds, the nervous patterns, or organization, or whatever name you wanted to give it, was present somewhere inside of me. I had been looking in the wrong place all of these years. What I wanted was on the inside, not on the outside. I resolved to put away my books and give up lessons, and somehow, teach myself.

The following winter, I returned to the mountains. I talked a few friends into trying my awareness exercises, with strange results. Some improved dramatically, others only a little. I myself had some flickers of my original breakthrough, but they were only dim shadows of the first time.

I became obsessed with these strange experiences. What was going on? How could I ski perfectly one minute and terribly the next? Why did the awareness exercises seem to work at some times, and not at others?

I realized that I had stumbled onto a puzzle. Gradually, I began to get a germ of an idea, and I began a search. As I searched I found clues to the solution of my puzzle from such disparate sources as an ancient system of metaphysics, and the most modern research in neurophysiology. I was on the trail of something. It was something that the ancient masters of Judo and Karate knew, I thought, and so must others, such as Nijinsky, the fabled Russian dancer. Others had these experiences, I found, and had written about them. But what triggered the experience? How did you get at it? That was the real question.

And always I skied. Finally, I gave up my field engineering job at sea just so I could ski four months every winter.

I had more breakthrough experiences, some more powerful than the first. Sometimes a strange kind of power would come on me, and I could make the most intricate moves on the steepest, most mogul-infested slopes, at high speed, while remaining in perfect balance. Falling seemed an impossibility.

Once, at the top of a steep, difficult bump run, I was blinded by a huge white light. When I could see again, I was at the bottom of the hill. Coming down was a dream, as if I had entered another dimension. The mountains seemed to shine around me with a strange light. My chest had turned to rubber, and I was breathing with a foreign rhythm.

And for days afterwards, I moved as if in a strange, peaceful trance.

I finally managed to go broke, skiing all winter and studying awareness all summer, and as a result I was unable to spend much time on the slopes for two years. But the mountains continued to call, and finally I was once again able to arrange to spend my winters skiing. Now the breakthroughs came with more and more regularity, and I felt that I was beginning to understand and use what it was in me that knew perfect movement. I decided to call my discovery the "Moving Mind," and I sat down to write a book. And since the key to working with the Moving Mind was learning to use the whole body in a particular way in every movement, the book would be called *Skiing with the Whole Body*.

PART I—

THE MOVING MIND

Why Johnny Can't Ski

The best skiers fly down the mountain with an ease and quality of movement that make the onlooker gasp with amazement. As his skis flash from side to side, and the snow flies in white cascades, the expert skier seems to be suspended by a magical thread somewhere between heaven and earth, in his own special world, as he dances with the mountain.

But very few skiers attain the expert, or even the advanced level of skiing. The vast majority of skiers get stuck somewhere in the intermediate range, and may go for years without any real improvement. Why do some people get stuck, and why do a few others seem to learn and improve so easily?

Until recently, there has been no real answer to this question. Most skiers were stuck at a low level of ability, while a fortunate few seemed to be gifted or blessed with some magical ability to learn how to ski. But research in neurophysiology over the last few decades has provided an answer.

To answer this question, "Why do a few people learn to ski easily while most get stuck and stop learning?" we must first understand how the brain, the nerves, the muscles, and the skeleton act to produce the movements that we must make to sit, stand, walk, run, and of course, to ski. When modern scientists first asked this question about a century ago, they came up with a fairly simple answer. When we move, a nerve cell fires somewhere in the brain, producing an impulse. The impulse is conducted down the nerve fiber, along the spinal cord, and then out to a muscle, which contracts to produce the desired movement.

All voluntary movement—which means the motions of our arms and legs, the turning of our head, the bending of our spine, and so on—was thought to be produced in this way. This idea seemed to provide a simple, straightforward explanation of how we move. The brain controls the muscles by sending nerve impulses down the spine.

The way that skiing is taught today (and most other physical activities, for that matter) reflects this model. Typically, the instructor demonstrates a move and explains what he is doing, pointing out various critical aspects of the motion, and then the student tries to copy the instructor's movement. Implicit in this approach is the idea that if we have a good understanding of the movement, we can, with a little practice, do it. That is, we can direct the right nerve cells in our brain to fire in such a way as to cause a particular motion, such as a parallel turn, to happen just as we would like it to.

However, in the middle part of this century, as the scientists began to probe deeper into the nervous systems of animals and humans, this simple model of how we control movement began to get more and more complex.

Today, the scientists who study brain functioning have identified a kind of overall scheme of organization of the human brain.

On the outside, upper part of the brain, just under the skull on the top and front of the head, are the structures that appear to be unique to human beings. This outer part of the brain, called the neocortex or new brain, is much more highly developed in humans than in any other animal.

As we penetrate deeper into the lower, inner parts of the brain, we find that our brains resemble somewhat the brains of certain other animals.

The neocortex is thought to be the seat of the uniquely human functions. The abilities that set us apart from other animals, such as playing a musical instrument, speaking and reasoning, doing mathematics, and so on, are thought to be located in this area. This part of the brain is the seat of the voluntary functions in humans. It is flexible in its workings and can be trained to think in different languages, to do mathematics, to compose music, learn to do accounting or plumbing, and so on.

The lower, inner parts of the brain, on the other hand, are considered to be the seat of the more automatic functions. These structures are responsible for our posture, breathing, balance, and the regulation of many of the automatic functions of the body. These parts of the brain are not directly subject to our voluntary control.

When scientists studying how the brain directs movement began to look closely at the nerve impulses arriving at the muscles, they discovered an amazing fact: the large majority of the nerve impulses arriving at the muscles originate in the inner, lower, automatic parts of the brain. That is, most of the nerve impulses arriving at the muscles are not under our voluntary control, and they work automatically, just like our heart pumps blood automatically, and just like we breathe automatically when we are asleep or unconscious.

This complex of automatic structures that control movement and are located mostly in the evolutionarily old part of the brain is so important that I have given it a name: I have called it the "Moving Mind." (Fig. 1)

The startling discovery that most of our movements are controlled automatically by the lower centers in the brain is the answer to the question that we posed earlier. A few, fortunate people manage to grow up with a well-organized Moving Mind. The majority of us do not. If the Moving Mind is well-organized, it is possible to learn to ski easily. If it is not, learning to ski well is practically impossible, *unless—unless* a way can be found to reorganize, or reprogram, the Moving Mind.

And that is the purpose of this book: To teach you to reprogram your Moving Mind so that you can become an expert skier.

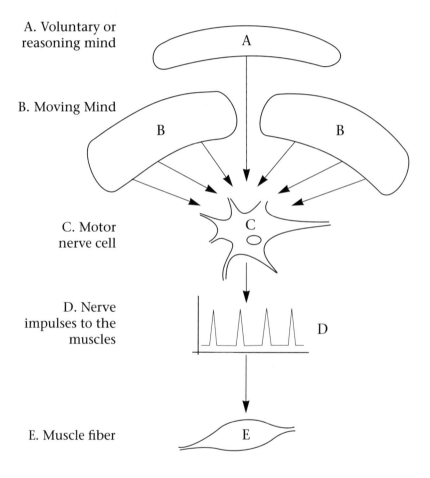

A. Voluntary or reasoning mind

B. Moving Mind

C. Motor nerve cell

D. Nerve impulses to the muscles

E. Muscle fiber

Figure 1. The Moving Mind
   Notice how the majority of the nerve impulses that control the muscles originate in the Moving Mind.

Experiencing
the Moving Mind

To experience some of the automatic functioning of the Moving Mind, try the following simple experiment. Stand in your normal standing posture. Begin to lean left and right, slowly, shifting your weight from one foot to the other. As you lean, pay attention to the feeling of pressure on the soles of your feet. As you lean to the left, the pressure increases on the sole of the left foot and decreases on the right; then, as you lean to the right, the pressure increases on the sole of the right foot and decreases on the left.

Lean left and right like this for several minutes. Start with a large movement, so that you shift almost all of your weight to each foot. Then gradually decrease the size of the shifting movement, until you can just barely feel the shift of pressure on the soles of the feet. Let yourself breathe easily as you move.

Stop moving and just stand still. Focus your attention on the soles of your feet and slowly lift your right arm straight out to the side. Notice what you feel on the soles of the feet as you lift your arm. Lift your arm five or six times.

When most people try this experiment, they feel that the weight does not shift on the soles of the feet. This is surprising at first thought, because lifting the right arm straight out to the side shifts the distribution of weight in the body to the right, and you might think that the pressure would shift over to the right foot a little, just as it did when you shifted your weight by leaning. Evidently, something else must be going on in the body to maintain balance when you lift your arm. This "something else" is the Moving Mind operating.

In every move we make, the distribution of weight in the body changes, even in moves as simple as lifting one arm to the side. In order to maintain balance, the muscles along the neck and spine, and around the pelvis and in the legs, must adjust to the altered weight distribution. Thus, when we "lift our arm," we are actually doing something with our *whole body*. Furthermore, the majority of the nerve impulses leaving the brain as we lift our arm are devoted to this maintenance of balance, and so they come from the Moving Mind. In almost any movement, then, the most important part of the movement occurs in the middle of the body, along the neck, spine, and pelvis, and is under the control of the Moving Mind.

Learning Ten Times Faster

All that we have said up to now is crucially important for down-hill skiing. In the middle of a parallel turn, most of your weight is balanced on a sliding surface that is just a fraction of an inch wide, and a few feet long. So balance is the critical issue, and thus any move that you make is almost completely controlled by the Moving Mind, which is responsible for balance.

When skiing at speed, the Moving Mind is responsible for about 90 to 95% of our movements. By working directly with the Moving Mind, then, we can speed up the process of learning to ski by a factor of ten to twenty times over that afforded by conventional instruction.

When we look at the typical intermediate skier moving with some speed down a fairly challenging slope, we can see the malfunctioning of the Moving Mind. The skier has almost no voluntary control. His entire body is stiff and is being run almost completely by the automatic systems—the Moving Mind—which haven't yet learned how to generate the movements required to slide down a slippery surface. There is just enough voluntary control for the skier to muscle his weight from one ski to another and back, and thereby force himself to turn just enough to avoid losing control altogether.

To get a feeling for what this means, tense your arm muscles very tightly, and write your name. You can do it, but it is difficult and tiring, and the results aren't very nice to look at. This is the situation with most skiers who have not yet learned to use their Moving Mind.

When the typical adult first gets on skis and begins to slide across the snow, the Moving Mind gets confused. Usually, the sensation of sliding like this signals to the Moving Mind that the body is out of control and is going to fall, and the Moving Mind does something to protect the body, such as waving the arms around to try to regain balance, or contracting the arms and legs and bending the spine so that if there is a fall, there will be less chance of injury. These two moves—waving the arms, and contracting the arms and legs and bending the spine— are commonly seen in many beginner and intermediate-level skiers. These are not really voluntary movements in the sense that we usually use these words, because the skier cannot control them at will. They are the product of the Moving Mind.

Reprogramming the Moving Mind

In order to be successful in skiing, the Moving Mind needs to be reprogrammed to deal with the novel situation of sliding without falling. If this is not done, instruction will be ineffective. The Moving Mind will be continuously taking over the movements of the body to try to regain balance, and the student will be fighting the Moving Mind—in effect, fighting himself—as he tries to learn to ski.

But because of the way the Moving Mind deals with movement, by involving the whole body, we must accomplish this reprogramming by learning to use the whole body in the most efficient way in every move that we make on skis. In practice, this means that when you are learning to edge your skis by moving your knees to the side, for example, you must also involve your hips, spine, ribs, neck and head in a certain way in the movement.

In skiing, the only voluntary part of a move is the decision to make the move. Once we have decided to turn, the automatic systems of the Moving Mind actually carry out the turn. Thus, to improve our skiing, we must work to improve the functioning of these automatic systems. That is what you will learn to do in this book.

The Reasoning Mind and the Moving Mind

The logical, reasoning mind, which you are using to read this book, thinks with words. Words are the building blocks of thought in this mind. The Moving Mind thinks with pressures, pictures, distances, and angles. These physical sensations are the building blocks of "thought" in this mind. Therefore, if we want to work with the Moving Mind, we must talk to it in its own language. That is what you will learn to do in this book. You will learn how to talk to your Moving Mind so that you can reprogram it in order to become an expert skier.

As I worked with myself and others, I found a simple way to think about the difference between talking to the Moving Mind and the intellectual or reasoning mind.

Traditionally, ski instructors have asked the question, "How should you ski?" Answering this question accesses the intellectual or reasoning mind and produces a *dictionary* of movements. It's useful for reference purposes, but it's not much good as a learning tool. (Have you ever tried to learn a foreign language from a dictionary?)

To access the Moving Mind, I found, the proper question is "How should you *learn* how to ski?"

The answer to this question accesses the Moving Mind, and leads to a *grammar* of movements.

Now we can see why so few people learn to ski well. Practically all ski instruction, both on the slopes and in books and articles, is directed to the reasoning mind. Once the student "understands" the movement—that is, once he can repeat the instructor's words back to him—he is expected to just do the movement. However, as we have seen, the reasoning mind has very little to do with the kind of fast movements involving critical balance situations that we find in skiing. When skiing at speed, the Moving Mind is practically running the body.

In fact, since most animals move so much better than we humans, and animals do not have the human reasoning power, we might expect that reason or understanding is actually a *hindrance* to proper movement. And many good skiers—including some top Olympic athletes—won't (or can't) describe and analyze how they ski. They do it by mainly by feeling—that is, mainly through the Moving Mind.

Besides, if "understanding" were really a help, physicists and mechanical engineers would make the best skiers, and that is hardly the case.

Nonetheless, most conventional lessons usually consist of the instructor analyzing the student's skiing, finding one or more problems in the student's technique, and then explaining to the student just what it is that he is doing wrong. Once the student "understands," he is then told to do something else. In practice, this usually means that the lesson consists of the instructor telling the student to do something that he is unable to do. Otherwise, he would not be there for the lesson.

Because of this, most instruction involves figuring out beforehand what you are supposed to do, and then trying to force your body into the pattern of movement that you think is correct, rather than just feeling out the easiest way for your body to move.

As infants, we learn so easily to sit, crawl, stand, walk and run, *not* by following the instructions of an expert, but rather by paying attention to ourselves as we move. As adults, we are so caught up with language that we forget this natural way of learning and become seduced by the clever verbal descriptions of "the experts." To some degree, even the popular video presentations of ski lessons can't evade this criticism.

There is one additional factor of great importance for reprogramming the Moving Mind. The nervous system mainly controls the muscles indirectly by altering the sensitivity of certain elements (called spindle cells) in the muscles that sense the length and tension of the muscle. Because of this, sensation and movement are inseparably linked. So, to improve our movements, we must improve our ability to sense how we are moving. For this reason, when working to reprogram our movements, we should make small, light, slow, easy movements so that we increase our sensitivity. In fact, the two elements of moving and sensing are so inseparably intertwined that we should make up a new word, such as "mensing," to connote *m*oving and *sensing,* to reflect the way the nervous system actually works.

In the following chapters you will find a method for reprogramming your Moving Mind to deal with the kind of movements involved in skiing at the expert level.

As you do this reprogramming, it is good to keep the following idea in mind. Although a good instructor is a great help in guiding your learning, especially in your first few days on the mountain, in the last analysis you must teach yourself. The reason for this is that only you can feel the pressure on the bottoms of your feet; only you can feel the tension in your muscles; only you can feel just how far your knees and hips are bent. Only you can tell if your skiing is what you really want it to be.

Because of this, the best method for learning to ski is one that takes into account the fact that each skier must take responsibility for his or her own learning, and that guides the skier towards increased awareness. Without awareness, the idea of "taking responsibility for your own learning" is just an empty phrase that taunts those who are having difficulty learning to ski. Any method that relies chiefly on a correct description handed down from above by "experts" is bound to produce very limited results.

The Safety Factor

Considering the speeds and forces involved, skiing is one of the safest sports. Nevertheless, injuries do sometimes occur in skiing. Skiing injuries are unusual in one particular way. Often, it is the beginner and intermediate skier who manage to injure themselves while falling at a speed of only five or ten miles per hour, while the expert may crash moving at three or four times that speed and be unhurt.

Why can the expert skier walk away from a fall at high speed while the beginner is sometimes injured by a fall at the speed of a slow run?

Skiing falls usually happen very quickly, and there is rarely any chance for the reasoning mind to direct the body to fall in a relaxed way. Movements during a fall are under the control of the Moving Mind. If the Moving Mind is holding the body stiff, as it does with most beginner and intermediate skiers, the chances of injury during a fall are greatly heightened. If, on the other hand, the Moving Mind has been reprogrammed correctly to deal with the kind of movements involved in skiing at speed, the body will be relaxed, and the force of the fall will be distributed over the whole body in such a way that no one part receives such a disproportionate amount of force that it causes an injury.

Therefore, learning to ski in a relaxed way leads to safer skiing.

The Method

Because this method of teaching downhill skiing grew out of my efforts to teach myself and others, I present it here as it was developed, as a series of stories.

Nevertheless, the awareness exercises in the stories are presented as a graded series, and at the end of each chapter there is a summary of the movements.

You will probably find that some of the exercises, especially the initial ones, seem a bit simplistic. However, the Moving Mind will learn many things from these simple movements, and after just a few hours you will find that you are beginning to do things on skis that you hardly dreamed were possible.

The Way of Skiing

Skiing, like the old martial arts, provides a way to take the complexities of life and reduce them to a manageable level—a level where it is possible to make the ephemeral parameters of life manifest in such a way that you can grapple with them and change them and so become more the kind of person you would like to be.

Like the ancient "ways" of the East—Judo, Karate-do and Aikido—skiing is a modern way, but with no opponent. As the old masters used to say, "The true opponent is yourself." In skiing, there is no possibility of confusion.

A Few Definitions

Downhill skiing has its own lexicon of special words, as do most sports. Following are the definitions of some common terms used by skiers. However, it is important to remember that a definition is just a series of words, and for the definition to be meaningful to you, you should be able to *see* and *feel* the "fall line," or be able to *do* or *recognize* a "stem turn" or a "parallel turn." If you do not already have a good idea of what most of these words mean, take a few lessons at an authorized ski school and find out before working with this book.

Beginner, Intermediate, Advanced, Expert: The continuum of skiing abilities is usually divided into these four categories. The Beginner usually uses a snow-plow or wedge turn, and stays on the easiest groomed slopes (marked with a green circle). The Intermediate uses a stem turn and skis the more difficult slopes (marked with a blue square). The Advanced skier uses a parallel turn, and skis the most difficult slopes (marked with a black diamond). Experts are usually racers or very good bump, tree, or powder skiers.

Snow-Plow or Wedge Turn: This is the first turn that all skiers learn. Even expert skiers use this turn to maneuver at slow speeds in close conditions, such as a lift line. In the wedge turn, the tips of the skis are held close together, and the tails far apart. The skier then pulls his knees together so that the inside edges of both skis are pushed into the snow, and turns the skis by shifting his weight from one ski to the other.

Stem Turn: This is an intermediate stage between the snow-plow and parallel turn. In a stem turn, the skier starts out with the skis parallel, opens them up into a wedge position during the turn, and then completes the turn with the skis parallel.

Parallel Turn: In a parallel turn, the skier turns the skis while keeping them close together and parallel to each other.

15

Tip, Tail, and Edge of the Ski: The tip of the ski, sometimes called the shovel, is in front; it is pointed and curved upward. The tail is the trailing edge of the ski, usually square and flat. The edges of the ski are the left and right corners between the bottom and side of the ski.

Edging or Edge Angle: The angle between the bottom of the ski and the snow surface. If the ski is flat on the snow, the edge angle is zero. As one edge lifts off the snow, the edge angle increases. Skiers set their uphill edges for control. Setting the downhill edge, called "catching an edge," usually results in a fall.

Bumps or Moguls: The regular rounded hillocks of snow produced by a large number of skiers skiing a slope.

Fall Line: Straight down the hill. To determine the fall line at any point, imagine that a ball is placed on the snow at that point and then released. The ball will roll in the direction of the fall line. If you stand with your skis perpendicular to the fall line, you will stand still. If your skis are pointed straight down the fall line, you will accelerate to terminal velocity. One of the ways that skiers control their speed is by controlling the angle that the skis make with the fall line. The closer the skis are to the direction of the fall line, the faster they go.

PART II—

THE LESSONS

1

Bill: Becoming Grounded

Although Bill had been skiing for five years, to look at him you would think that he had only been skiing for five minutes.

He had the typical first day beginner's stance. He was pitched forward so that his torso was almost parallel to the ground, and his entire body appeared stiff as a board. He looked more like a concrete statue on skis than a human being. As soon as his skis started to move over the snow, he would pitch forward and remain immobile in this awkward position. His face was rigid, his jaw clamped, and his shoulders pulled up almost to the level of his ears. I couldn't believe that he had started skiing five years ago.

Bill had tried lessons and books, but nothing really seemed to help his skiing much. We had met a few days earlier, through a mutual friend, and he had become curious about my awareness approach to ski instruction. We made an appointment to try it out, and now the time had come.

But what was I going to do with Bill? At first glance, he seemed like a hopeless case. *Everything* seemed to be wrong with his technique. I was sure that if I just tried to correct the details, telling him to stand straight, drop his shoulders, and breathe, relax, and so on, we would accomplish nothing. Anyway, instructors and friends had certainly been telling him those things for years.

There had to be some key element, some root cause, of Bill's inability to learn to ski. What one thing could cause Bill to have so many problems?

I skied up to Bill and told him to stop. With what appeared to be a stupendous effort, he maneuvered his skis around so

19

that he was going across the fall line, and so he stopped. He stood up straight and let out a huge sigh. Apparently, he had been holding his breath all that time! I wondered what kind of determination he had to persist at skiing for five years when he had to put that much effort into it.

Watching Bill "ski," I had the impression that he wasn't grounded, or that he didn't feel as if he had a firm place on which to stand. Anyone who feels ungrounded will bend over and tighten himself up like Bill was doing. I guessed that he might be lacking an awareness of what was happening on the soles of his feet. If he didn't feel that he had a solid base to stand on, he would almost certainly be stiff and awkward on his skis. I decided to work on bringing some awareness to his feet and thereby improve his skiing.

I asked Bill to bring his skis fairly close together, so that they were parallel and at right angles to the fall line. I asked him if he felt fairly comfortable and safe standing still like that, and he said that he did.

Then, I asked him to lean forward and back, and to pay attention to the sensation of the pressure shifting forward and back on the soles of his feet. He looked at me with a mildly curious expression, as if I had used a word that he didn't understand.

I demonstrated, leaning my body forward and back a few times. "Do that," I said, "and just feel how the pressure shifts from your toes to your heels as you move."

Bill leaned forward and back several times, then stopped and looked at me. "I don't feel a thing," he said.

"You mean that you can't feel *anything* on the bottoms of your feet as you lean forward and back?" I asked incredulously.

"No," he repeated, "I can't feel anything at all down there."

My impression about Bill had been right. Something about the situation of skiing had caused him to withdraw his awareness from the soles of his feet. Without any feeling at all from the bottoms of his feet, he would be unable to balance himself efficiently. Feeling that he was unable to balance, and that he was going to fall, he pitched forward and stiffened his body. This is a problem that besets practically all skiers to some extent.

Bill, however, was the first skier I had met who was completely unable to feel the bottoms of his feet. It made sense, though. I had never seen anyone who had been skiing for five years who was as stuck as Bill.

But now I was in a quandary. If Bill couldn't feel anything on the bottoms of his feet, I would be unable to do what I wanted to with him, which was to get him to feel how the pressure shifted on the soles of his feet as he leaned forward and back. Finally I had an idea.

"Loosen all of the buckles on one boot," I told him, "so that your foot can move around easily inside your boot." Bill leaned over and loosened the buckles on his right boot.

"Now," I said, "lift your heel up inside the boot, and set it back down, and try to feel your heel touch the boot."

Bill began to move his right foot up and down. He had a look of intense concentration on his face. Suddenly he stopped moving, his face brightened, and he looked at me and said, "Yeah, I can feel it now."

"OK," I said, "lean forward and back, and as you lean forward lift up your heel, and as you lean back, set it down, and pay attention to that."

Bill leaned forward and back a few times. "I'm starting to feel what you're talking about now," he reported. "It feels real strange somehow."

"Keep doing that," I said, "and don't lift your heel. Just feel how the pressure increases and decreases as you lean forward and back."

Bill continued to lean forward and back. "I can feel it on my heel and . . . hey . . . I can feel it on the front of my foot, too. I don't think I feel that when I ski," he added.

"Buckle up your boot," I told Bill, "and try it like that."

Bill snapped his buckles down and began to lean forward and back. "Yeah," he reported, "I can still feel it."

"How about the other foot?" I asked.

"Yep. I can feel it there too," he replied.

"All right," I said, "do that while you are skiing very slowly across the slope, at about the speed that you walk."

As soon as Bill started to move, he pitched forward and separated his skis, and pulled his shoulders up toward his ears. Somehow, though, he managed to lean forward and back a little, and I guessed from the look of intense concentration on his face that he was trying to feel the shift of pressure on the bottoms of his feet. I followed close behind him.

Bill went about 200 feet across the slope like that. Suddenly he stopped, stood up straight, and looked around at me.

"Damn it!" he said, with great force.

"What's the matter?" I asked, concerned.

"I've been skiing for five years and I never felt the bottoms of my feet. No wonder I couldn't ski!" Bill had made the intuitive connection that the lack of awareness in his feet was the major cause of his inability to learn to ski.

"That's crazy," he added. "Trying to ski without feeling is like trying to draw without seeing. Why didn't somebody show me this before?

"But what do I do now?" he asked. "Just ski and try to feel my feet?"

"That won't work," I told him. "As soon as you start to ski, you lock yourself into your old habits, and those habits include withdrawing your awareness from the soles of your feet. We need to develop your awareness slowly, and then integrate it into your skiing."

"So how do I do that?"

"Just keep skiing very slowly across the slope, and lean forward and back, like you were doing. As you move, feel the pressure shift on the bottoms of your feet, and also scan your body with your attention, so that you can feel what each part is doing to make the pressure move forward and backward. When you get to the side of the trail, stop, turn around, and then come back the other way."

Bill turned around and began to ski slowly across the slope, still leaning forward and back. Before my eyes an incredible transformation began. Bill started to stand up straighter, his shoulders began to drop down, and he began to breathe. His whole body loosened up, and he started to look more like a human being than a statue.

After about ten minutes of traverses, Bill came to a stop beside me. "It's good," he said. "I can feel the pressure go all the way from the front to the back of my foot."

"Well then, what do you do with your toes?" I asked him.

"My toes? I don't know."

"Just keep leaning forward and back and feel what your toes are doing," I told him.

Bill continued to lean. "I can't really feel them," he said.

"Just keep doing it for a minute and it will come in," I replied.

After about a minute Bill said, "It feels like I'm curling my toes up against the bottoms of my boots as I lean forward. Is that right?"

"It doesn't surprise me," I told him. "Now here's what's next. Just do that same thing, skiing slowly across the trail, but as you lean forward, curl your toes up even more, so that they press strongly into the bottom of the boot. Relax them as you lean back."

After a few minutes Bill motioned me over to him. "When I curl my toes it feels like I stiffen my whole body," he said.

"That's right," I told him. "I want you to feel that stiffening so that you can let go of it."

He continued to ski slowly across the trail, leaning forward and back. After a few minutes I had him do the same thing, except now I asked him to lift his toes up as he leaned forward.

We spent about 45 minutes getting the feel of shifting the weight forward and back while skiing. At the end of that time Bill was standing almost perfectly straight and relaxed as he moved across the slope.

"Hey," I said, "come over here by me." He did a quick, sharp, snow-plow turn and stopped facing me. "Wow," he said, "that's incredible!" Now that he was standing up fairly straight, and had let go of some of the excess tension in his muscles, turning was a lot easier.

I agreed. I had never seen such a big change happen so quickly. On the other hand, I had never seen anyone who was so completely unable to feel what was happening on the bottoms of their feet as Bill had been.

With such a powerful learning experience under his belt, Bill began to progress rapidly. In another two days, he was doing good stem turns, and I told him that if he could arrange to spend another ten or fifteen days on the hill that season, he should be able to do full parallel turns on an easy slope without much trouble.

Bill was an extreme example of something that affects almost every skier to some extent. In the novel situation of being on skis for the first time, we somehow manage to shut off much of our sensory input. Without awareness in our feet, we feel ungrounded and out of balance. Learning to ski well without being able to feel what is happening in our bodies is impossible. Without being able to feel what we are doing, we can't do what we want. However, once we become aware of what we are doing, the improvement is practically automatic.

Summary

Here is a summary of what I did with Bill. As you try these movements yourself, be sure to move slowly and easily, and to scan your body with your attention, noticing any stiff spots. Pay particular attention to making sure you do not hold your breath. Spend at least ten minutes on each movement.

1. Find a wide, flat, beginner or easy intermediate-level slope. Stand at the side of the trail, facing out across it. Bring your skis together, with the uphill ski leading a little, and bend your knees. Ski very slowly across the hill, while leaning forward and then back to center. Feel how the weight on the soles of your

Fig 1–1

feet shifts forward toward your toes, and then back. When you reach the side of the trail, stop, turn around, and ski back the other way. Start each traverse with your skis together, but don't force your skis to stay together after you start moving. As your awareness grows, you will find that your skis stay together without you having to think about it. (Fig 1–1)

2. Ski very slowly across the hill while leaning backward and then back to center. Feel how the weight on your soles shifts backward toward your heels, and returns to center. (Fig 1–2)

Fig 1–2

3. Now combine the two previous movements by skiing slowly across the hill while leaning forward and backward. Feel how your weight shifts along the soles of your feet. As you feel your weight shift, scan your body with your attention and notice what you do with your ankles, your knees, your hips, your torso, and your head to shift the pressure forward and back. (Fig 1–3A/B)

Fig 1–3A   *Fig 1–3B*

4. Repeat the previous movement, leaning forward and backward, and feel your toes. Exactly what do your toes do as you lean forward? (Fig 1–4A/B)

Fig 1–4A

Fig 1–4B

5. Ski slowly across the hill while leaning forward and back, and as you lean forward, curl your toes so that they push down into the bottom of the boot. As you lean back, relax your toes. What happens in your body as you curl your toes? Do you stiffen any part? Do you hold your breath? (Fig 1–5A/B)

Fig 1–5A

Fig 1–5B

6. Ski slowly across the hill while leaning forward and back. As you lean forward, lift your toes up so that they press into the top of the boot. Relax your toes as you lean back. (Fig 1–6A/B)

Fig 1–6A

Fig 1–6B

7. Ski slowly back and forth across the hill while leaning forward and back, and just feel the pressure shift from your heels to your toes and back. Can you feel the pressure shift easily all along the soles now? What do your toes do now as you lean forward? Remember to scan your body from your feet to your head as you move. (Fig 1–7A/B)

Fig 1–7A

Fig 1–7B

2

Bev: Learning Without Teaching

Bev was one of my very first students. She had had about two weeks of skiing experience over the previous three years, and was still a beginner. She did a snow-plow turn stiffly, but without too much effort. She still had the typical "beginner's stance," with her body pitched forward, so that her torso was at a 45-degree angle to the ground.

The first time I got on the lift with Bev, she grabbed the center pole with both hands and held on for dear life. I started to kid her about falling off the lift.

"It's not funny," she said through clenched teeth.

I realized that it *wasn't* funny, at least to Bev. As we rode up, I started to wonder how I was going to teach someone to ski if they were petrified just riding the lift.

"Well," I thought to myself, "it can't hurt to try."

I spent about an hour that morning working with Bev, having her lean forward and back while feeling the pressure shift on the bottoms of her feet. She seemed to loosen up a little, but I couldn't see any real change in her skiing. I was a bit disappointed.

The next morning I spent another hour working with Bev, this time having her feel the pressure shift on her feet as she did some other movements. Again, there wasn't much change in her skiing. I was a little more disappointed.

On the third morning, I decided to work with tilting the feet from side to side. This "edging" is a critical movement for skiers, and oftentimes an improvement here produces a dramatic change in skiing ability.

"Stop here at the side of the trail," I told Bev, "and climb up this steep section about a foot. I want to show you something."

Bev sidestepped up a small but steep embankment a few feet, so that her skis were on a small section of trail that had a 45-degree pitch.

"Now," I said, "lift your downhill ski up off the snow a little and then set it back down so that you put your full weight on the ski."

Bev began to lift her ski up and then set it down.

"Feel what the ski does just as it contacts the snow and you put your weight on it," I told her.

Bev continued to move for about a minute, then she looked at me and said, "It doesn't do anything. It just moves up and down. I don't think I understand what you mean."

"Keep doing that and *watch* the ski. Tell me what you see."

Bev kept moving, and watched the ski intently. "It tilts a little as I put my weight on it. It that what you mean?"

"That's exactly what I mean. As you set your weight onto the ski and it contacts the snow surface, the downhill edge of the ski drops down a little. And you could see it, but you couldn't feel it. Do you know what that means?" I asked.

"No," she said.

"It means that your skis are moving around without you being able to feel them. If you can't feel what your skis are doing, you can't control them."

"So what are we going to do about that?" Bev asked.

"Come over here and I'll show you."

We stopped at the edge of the trail and I told Bev what I wanted her to do. "Ski very slowly across the trail and just tilt your skis so that you feel the pressure on the bottoms of your feet shift toward the uphill edge. Then, relax and let the pressure come back to center."

Bev began to move slowly across the trail, tilting her feet as I had directed. I had her go back and forth across the trail for several minutes until the movement looked easy and fluid.

"Now," I said, "do the same thing except this time tilt your skis so that the pressure moves toward the downhill edge. Don't tilt too much or you'll start to slide sideways."

Once again I watched until the movement appeared easy and relaxed.

"Now, one more thing. Just combine those two movements so that you tilt your skis left and right. Be sure to feel how the pressure on your feet shifts from the left side of each foot to the right and back. And be sure to scan your body from head to toe as you move, so that you can feel if you are holding any part stiff."

Bev began to ski slowly across the slope and I followed behind. After a few minutes I began to direct her attention to some other parts of her body. I asked her to notice how her knees moved from side to side as she shifted her weight. Then I asked her to notice what she could feel in her hips, her spine, her ribs, and finally her head and neck. As she let her attention move through her body she began to spontaneously relax, and I could see that she could do the movement easily.

I found another short section of steep terrain for her to stand on and had Bev repeat the movement of lifting her downhill ski and then setting it back down on the snow and letting her full weight come onto the ski. "Can you feel the ski tilt now?" I asked.

"Yep," she said, "no problem."

"Go ski a little," I told her. "I want to see what's happened to your style."

I watched Bev ski down the slope. I had hoped for something dramatic, but still, there was hardly any change in her skiing. I was really disappointed. I began to think I was completely on the wrong track with my ideas about learning to ski. Whatever had happened to me when I had my breakthrough had been some peculiarity of my own personal organization, and it wouldn't work for anyone else.

The next day I had something to do in the morning, and I arranged to meet Bev at a certain spot on the hill at one o'clock.

I got to the meeting place just before one. It was mid-week, and there were hardly any other skiers around. As I stood there, I watched a lone skier coming down the hill toward me. She

30

stood perfectly upright, and did a series of crisp, sharp stem turns. I admired her form. She skied up beside me and stopped. It was Bev!

I was flabbergasted. The day before, Bev had been crouched over her skis and was putting a lot of effort into her beginner's snow-plow turn. Suddenly, one day later, she was standing up right and doing an excellent intermediate-level stem turn. She appeared to have progressed two or three months overnight. I felt something slipping inside my head. What was going on?

I pulled myself together. "Well," I said to Bev, "you must be really pleased with your stem turn."

Bev gave me a blank look. "What's a stem turn?" she asked.

Now I really felt disoriented. "What do you mean, 'What's a stem turn?'" I demanded. "It's what you were just doing, skiing down here. Can't you feel the difference?"

"Oh, yeah, it feels easier to ski today, if that's what you mean," Bev replied. "But I still don't know anything about a 'stem turn.'"

"Look," I said, "to do a stem turn, you push the tail of the uphill ski out away from the tail of the downhill ski as you turn down toward the fall line, and then you shift your weight over to your uphill ski, and finally you bring the tail of the downhill ski, which is now the uphill ski, because you've just turned, back close to the tail of the downhill ski, and come up on the other traverse."

"That sounds *complicated,*" said Bev. "I could never do that!"

"But that's what you were just doing, skiing down here to meet me," I said excitedly.

"Oh," Bev said. "I guess that's good, huh?"

"Ah, you might say that," I replied.

I felt like I needed some time to digest what had happened. Bev had a tremendous breakthrough into a whole new level of skiing, and she didn't know what she was doing. I had never mentioned the words 'stem turn' to her, and yet here she was doing it as if she had been born on skis.

"Look," I said, "let's blow off the lesson today. Why don't you just ski around and enjoy the mountain."

I turned to go. I had just skied a few feet when a strange idea popped into my mind, seemingly out of nowhere. I stopped and turned to Bev.

"Hey," I said, "ski down to the lift and ride up with me. I want to talk to you about something."

The base of the lift was just a little ways down the hill. We skied down and got on. Bev settled back against the back rest comfortably. Her hands were resting in her lap, instead of holding onto the center pole. It was the same lift we had ridden on the first day.

"Aren't you afraid you might fall?" I said. "Shouldn't you hold onto the pole?"

"Oh, ah, the lift doesn't seem so high today. What did you want to talk about, anyway?"

"Oh, it was nothing, really. I can't remember now. Must not have been that important."

At the top of the lift we got off, and I watched Bev ski off down the hill, with her perfect 'stem turns' that she didn't know how to do. I tried to ski, but my head was so full of questions that I couldn't pay attention to what I was doing. I skied down to the base, took off my skis, and went home.

I spent hours thinking about what had happened to Bev, and it actually took me several years to arrive at an adequate explanation of how she could learn a stem turn without being taught how to do it.

The problem I had understanding Bev's experience came from the way I had been taught to think about learning, and in particular about learning to ski. In almost all the skiing instructional books I had read, and in all the lessons I had taken, great emphasis was placed on having the student understand the technique that was to be learned.

To this end an elaborate explanation was offered, and a series of pictures of an expert demonstrating the technique was presented. One book went so far as to present what a physicist would call a "force vector diagram," showing a skier in the middle of a parallel turn, with the various force vectors resolved into their horizontal and vertical components, and explaining how the resultant force vector should strike the earth inside the area of support. The diagram and explanation were impressive, but I wondered how many of my skiing friends could solve a force vector diagram. Since I had studied physics, I knew that I could do it, but not while in the middle of a parallel turn.

The tacit assumption behind this method of teaching by explanation and demonstration is that if the student understands what he is to do, then with a little practice, he will be able to do it. This method of teaching fits the old, outmoded theory of 80 years ago of how the brain functions. In light of current neurological research, it doesn't make sense. What I discovered by working with Bev, and later with others, is that not only is a detailed explanation of little use, but in most cases it actually *impedes* the learning process.

As I thought about Bev, I began to get an idea. She had learned to do a stem turn, which was a big advance for her, without being able to explain in words what she was doing. How could that be possible? Evidently the part of the brain that thinks in words was not the part that had organized her body to do the turn. Therefore, I reasoned, there must be another part of the brain that deals with movement and is able to figure out how to do a stem turn without Bev's intellectual understanding.

Thinking back, I realized that I had done the same thing to myself a few years before. However, I had spent a lot of time thinking and analyzing my skiing, and I knew intellectually what I needed to do to make a parallel turn, even though I couldn't actually do it very well. When I had my big breakthrough, I assumed that somehow my intellectual understanding had penetrated into my body, so that I could suddenly ski.

But now, after watching Bev, I realized that assumption was wrong. The intellectual understanding had very little to do with it.

Thus, I realized that there is another mind hidden away somewhere deep inside of each of us, a special part of the mind that deals with movement. Slowly, I began to think of this part as the "Moving Mind."

Therefore, I reasoned, teaching a parallel turn by means of explanation is something like trying to improve the function of the heart by explaining how the heart works, and then telling the student, "Make your heart beat faster!"

It is, of course, impossible to speed up the heart in this way. However, it *is* possible to speed up the heart indirectly, by running for some distance. In a similar manner, it is possible to influence the involuntary part of the nervous system that deals with movement, which I call the Moving Mind, in an indirect way.

My experience with Bev showed me how powerful changes can be made in someone's skiing ability just by having them feel how they are moving. And something else happened with Bev, also. As a result of whatever changed in her nervous system to enable her to stand up straight on skis and do a stem turn, she lost her fear of riding on the lift. In fact, she actually changed her perception of the height of the lift, and now, she says, "It doesn't seem so high."

Summary

Here's what I did with Bev to help her improve. As you try these movements yourself, remember to move slowly and easily and to avoid any kind of effort, so that you can feel all the subtle details of what you are doing. As the movement becomes easier, scan your body from feet to head with your attention as you move. Just feel what each part is doing to make the tilting movement. Spend about ten minutes on each movement.

Fig 2-1

1. First, test your ability to feel the tilting movement of the skis. Stand still on a steep section of trail and lift your downhill ski a few inches off the snow. Then, slowly set it back down onto the

snow, and put your full weight onto the ski. As you do this, try to feel with your foot what the ski does. After a few trials, look down at the ski. You will be able to see that the downhill edge of the ski drops down as you set the ski slowly onto the snow. Keep raising and lowering the ski until you can feel the tilting movement of the ski with your foot without looking at it. (Fig 2–1)

2. Now, find a wide, flat beginner or easy intermediate-level slope. Bring your skis together, uphill ski leading a little, and bend your knees. Start each traverse with your skis together, but don't force your skis to stay together after you start to move. Begin to ski slowly across the slope at about the speed that you walk. As you move across the slope, tilt your skis so that your weight moves onto the uphill side of each foot. Then relax and let your weight come back to center. As the movement becomes easy, scan your body with your attention. Notice what you do with your knees, your hips, your torso, your shoulders, and your head. Do you hold your breath as you do the movement? (Fig 2–2)

Fig 2–2

3. Continue to ski slowly across the slope but this time tilt your skis so that the pressure on the bottoms of your feet moves toward the downhill edges of the skis, and then relax and let the pressure come back to center. If your skis start to slide sideways down the hill, reduce the amount of tilting. Continue to feel how the pressure shifts on the soles of your feet as you scan your body with your attention. (Fig 2–3)

Fig 2–3

4. Now combine the two previous movements so that you shift your weight left and right across the soles of your feet. Continue to do this as you ski slowly across the slope and scan your body with your attention. (Fig 2–4A/B)

Fig 2–4A   Fig 2–4B

5. Now find a short steep section of hill and repeat the very first movement, raising and lowering the downhill ski while feeling how the ski tilts as you set it onto the snow. Can you feel the ski tilt clearly now? Make a few turns on an easy section of the hill and notice how your turns feel now that you have increased your awareness of how your body moves to cause the pressure to shift from side to side on the soles of your feet.

3

Maria: The Coordinate System on the Feet

Maria was a friend of mine from down in the flatlands. One day in the fall we were chatting and I began to talk about my plans to ski that winter. Maria got a wistful look in her eyes and said, "I used to ski a lot, but I haven't been in almost 15 years."

"Why did you stop?" I asked.

"Well, I skied a lot, as much as I could, in grade school and high school. But then I moved down here, and it was just too much trouble to go."

"Well, I'll tell you what," I told Maria, "Come up skiing this winter and I'll get you back into it."

We made plans, and Maria flew up to Colorado. Unfortunately, the evening she arrived I came down with a particularly virulent case of the flu. By the next morning, I could hardly walk down stairs, and skiing was out of the question. I explained the first series of exercises, leaning forward and back, and then drove Maria up to the ski area. I pointed out the rental shop, and then drove home and collapsed. The second day was almost a repeat of the first, except that I had Maria tilt her skis left and right.

That evening I felt a little better, and we had a discussion about the two exercises.

"I can feel that something is happening to my skiing. It's getting a little easier, but I don't understand why you want me to do those weird exercises. I've had a lot of ski instruction, and I never did anything like that," Maria told me.

Maria was an engineer, and I knew that she would respond to an intellectual explanation, so I decided to give her one. I got a pen and piece of paper, and handed it to her. "Draw me a graph of the function y equals x squared plus one, from x equals minus three to plus three."

Maria looked at me and frowned. "What's that got to do with skiing?" she asked.

"Just try it. I want to show you something."

Maria started by drawing two lines at right angles to make the '+' figure of the Cartesian coordinate system that we all learn to use to draw graphs in high school algebra. She started to figure the x and y values for the graph, but I stopped her.

"Wait a second," I said. "Remember when you shifted the pressure forward and back, and then left and right on your feet? If you were to draw a 'graph' of how the pressure shifted along your feet, what would it look like?"

Maria thought about my question for a few seconds. "The forward and back movement would be like an up-and-down line on the paper," she said, drawing a line, "and the left and right movement would be a left-and-right line on the paper." She drew a second line intersecting the first at right angles. The figure she had drawn was identical to the Cartesian coordinate system that she had drawn earlier. I pointed this out to her. She looked back and forth at the two figures a few times, and then her face brightened.

"I see what you're doing," she said. "You're making a coordinate system on the bottoms of my feet so I can shift my weight to any direction I want."

"Right," I replied. "Once you can shift your weight easily in the right-and-left and forward-and-back directions, you can shift anywhere in between by just combining those two movements, just like you can draw the graph of any function by using the Cartesian coordinate system.

"So here's what you do tomorrow. Repeat the forward-and-back, and left-and-right movements a few times, until you can get a clear feeling that the point of maximum pressure shifts on the soles of your feet in such a way as to form a '+' figure. Then you can experiment with other kinds of shifts. Be sure to try a circle, with the center of the circle at the center of the 'coordinate system.' Since a circle contains all directions, if you can shift your weight easily in a circle, you will have complete freedom to shift your weight however you need to as you ski.

"Now here's the really important part: If you find some parts of the circle where it is difficult to shift your weight, just go very slowly, and watch your breathing, and check to make sure that you haven't tightened your shoulders, or set your jaw, or something like that. If you find a part of the circle that is difficult to move through, you can bet that you are tensing up some part of your body without realizing it."

Maria jumped up and took off her shoes. "I'm going to try it right now," she said, and began to lean this way and that.

"It's OK to do it now, but be sure to repeat the whole thing tomorrow with skis on, since you can lean much further forward and back with the skis to balance you."

The next day I still didn't feel like skiing, so I again drove Maria up to the hill. At 4:30 I drove back and picked her up.

"You're not going to believe what happened to me today," she said with a big smile, as she got into the car. "I started doing what you had told me, shifting my weight this way and that and feeling the pressure shift on the bottoms of my feet. After a while I realized that I had always constricted myself while I was skiing. I always kept my weight centered right in the middle of that 'coordinate system.' Once I felt that I could move, shift my weight wherever I wanted to, my skiing changed drastically. In fact, I just started doing parallel turns without even trying. What a fantastic feeling!"

My flu lasted for several more days, and I never got to ski with Maria that winter. But every time I see her she talks about how the 'coordinate system' fixed her skiing.

Summary

Here's what I did with Maria to help her improve. As you try these exercises remember to move slowly so that you can feel all the details of each movement, and how your body is moving to cause the pressure to shift on the soles of your feet.

1. Find a wide, flat beginner or easy intermediate slope. Bend your knees and bring your skis together with the uphill ski leading. Begin to ski slowly across the slope. As you move, repeat the exercise from the first day of leaning forward and back. Feel how the pressure shifts from your heels to your toes and back as you lean. Notice how the point of maximum pressure describes a line along the bottom of each foot from the heel to the toes. When you get to the other side of the trail, stop, turn around, and try it going back on the other traverse. (Fig 3–1A/B)

Fig 3–1A   Fig 3–1B

2. Now repeat the exercise from the second day, shifting the pressure from left to right across the bottoms of your feet while going slowly across the slope. (Fig 3–2A/B) Notice how the point of maximum pressure describes a line at right angles to the first line, so that the two lines together form a '+' figure.

Fig 3–2A   *Fig 3–2B*

3. Stand still at the side of the trail, skis together and knees bent. Shift your weight forward and back a few times, and then left and right, until you can clearly feel the '+' figure on the bottoms of your feet. Then, begin to shift your weight in such a way as to draw a circle centered on the middle of the '+.' Move slowly and pay careful attention to the shape of the circle. Is it a perfect circle? If you find a part of the circle that is difficult or unclear, or where the circle is flat, go through that part very slowly and direct your attention to different parts of your body. When you find where you are stiffening yourself, you will be able to make the whole circle clearly. Try a small circle, and then a larger one. Finally, make the circle while skiing slowly across the trail.

4

Mark: Moving and Sensing

I had been working with Mark for several days, and he was progressing well. I placed his skiing ability between beginner and intermediate. He had just started to do a stem turn when the conditions were easy, but the turn was slow and still fairly awkward.

It was our fourth session on the mountain, and I felt that Mark needed to improve the way he sensed how the pressure on the bottoms of his feet affected what his skis were doing. I had already worked with him before on this, and now I decided to do a little more.

Mark and I skied over to a wide, flat, beginner's trail. I had him stand at the side of the trail with his skis perpendicular to the fall line, and facing out onto the trail. It was a beautiful, clear day, and we both were silent for a minute as we looked out at the snow-covered mountain tops framed by the bright blue sky. I felt really lucky to be alive.

I brought my attention back to Mark. "Tell me something. What percentage of your weight do you have on each ski while you're skiing?"

He was silent for a few seconds, and then he frowned and said, "I'm not really sure. How much weight am I supposed to have on each ski, anyway?"

It is agreed among skiers that most of a skier's weight should be on the downhill ski. Some say the percentage should be 60/40, others say 70/30, or even 80/20. Some skiers even lift their uphill ski as they turn so that 100% of the weight is on the downhill ski. Of course when actually skiing there can be considerable variation in the weight distribution from one second to the next. Also, when skiing straight down the hill, about half of the weight is on each ski.

However, this information is not of much use to a skier who is unable to feel how much weight is on each ski.

I explained weight distribution to Mark, and told him that I was going to help him learn to feel how shifting his weight from one ski to another affected his skiing. Then he could experiment and find out what kind of weight distribution worked for him.

When you learn in this way, the kind of knowledge that you get is *qualitatively* different from the learning obtained by just reading the opinion of this or that 'expert.' One kind of learning is just a series of words memorized. The other is in your bones, where it counts.

"Just begin to shift your weight from one ski to the other," I told Mark. "Shift it all the way, so that you actually lift each ski up off the snow about an inch. As you do that, just feel how the pressure shifts on the bottoms of your feet."

Mark began to shift his weight from side to side.

"Let yourself breathe easily, and just scan your body with your attention as you move. That way, you can discover if you are holding any parts stiff without knowing it."

After about a minute of this, I asked Mark to continue the shifting movement while skiing very slowly across the slope. I had him go across and back many times, until I could see that he was doing the movement without straining any part of his body, or holding his breath.

I caught up with Mark. "Remember a couple of lessons ago when I had you shift your weight from side to side so that your skis tilted left and right?" I asked. Mark said that he remembered.

"Well, what's the difference between this movement that you just did and the one of shifting your weight so that the skis tilt from side to side? They are different movements, but both involve some kind of side-to-side motions. What do you do with your body to produce the two movements?"

Mark opened his mouth as if about to ask a question, paused, and then closed his mouth. He began to shift his weight so as to tilt his skis left and right. I could tell from the faraway look in his eyes that he was concentrating on the internal sensations of movement and trying to feel what differentiated the two movements. In one movement the total weight shifts from ski to ski. In the other, the weight is balanced almost equally on each ski, but the skis tilt from left to right. I could see Mark try first one movement, then the other, as he tried to discover the exact difference.

Watching Mark, I was really pleased. If I can give my students the idea that they can learn *from themselves,* by moving and experimenting with their own bodies, then the way is wide open for them to learn to ski at a very high level. For me, this idea that you can learn from yourself is the single most important feature that distinguishes those who learn to ski quickly and easily from those who become 'permanent intermediates.' Mark had been about to ask me what the difference was but had suddenly decided to find the answer himself.

After a few minutes his face brightened, and he stopped moving. "I know what it is," he said.

He told me the difference. "I couldn't have said it better myself," I told him.

We had been working about an hour. "Why don't you make a few runs, and I'll come look for you early this afternoon to see how you are doing," I said.

Mark took off down the beginner's trail, and I cut over to another lift so that I could get my "bump ration" for the day.

After a few hours, I had thoroughly scrambled my brains on the steep bump runs, and I headed back over to the beginner's trail to check on Mark.

I stopped at the top of the trail and looked down the hill. There was Mark, about halfway down. I skied down and began to follow him, watching his skiing.

He had made a big change in his technique, I could see. His stem turn had improved dramatically from that morning. In fact, he was almost doing a parallel turn. There was just a hint of the tails of the skis separating during the turn. Also, he looked a lot more solid and stable on his skis.

I yelled at Mark to stop, and skied up beside him. "Looks pretty good," I said. "What does it feel like to you?"

"It's dynamite," he said, with a big smile on his face, "but let me tell you what happened.

"After you left I kept skiing, and my toes started to feel real funny. I can't say exactly what I felt, but something was changing there, and my attention kept being drawn to my toes. I got so involved with my toes I think I went into a trance. Anyway, one time I skied all the way down the trail, and when I got to the lift, I couldn't remember skiing down.

"Finally, whatever was going on in my toes finished, and I noticed that my skiing was real different. It sure feels nice. What happened, anyway? I've never felt anything like that before."

"I'm sure you learned like that when you were very young," I told Mark, "but you've probably forgotten the feeling. To tell you the truth, I don't know a whole lot more about it than you do. What I *do* know is how to get that kind of improvement. Exactly what goes on in the body is anyone's guess.

"However, there is one clue. Neurophysiologists have discovered that moving and sensing are inextricably linked in the nervous system. You can't move effectively without sensing, and you can't sense without moving, and in fact it's only in words that you can talk about 'moving' and 'sensing' as if they were two different activities. So in order to make a real change in your movement, you have to change the way you *feel* yourself and the world."

"That makes sense," said Mark, "and it sure feels terrific. I can't believe what I'm doing. It's like magic."

"I'll talk to you later," he said, turning to start down the hill. "I don't want to waste time while the lifts are running."

Later that evening I saw Mark in the lodge. He was standing in his ski boots and talking to some friends. I noticed another change. Good skiers have a very relaxed way of standing in their ski boots with their knees bent. The high, stiff ski boot keeps the knee from bending all the way, and the skier can stand almost as if he or she is leaning against a support. Those without much skiing experience usually stand with their knees almost straight, which is somewhat awkward in most modern ski boots. Standing there, with his knees relaxed and bent, Mark looked every inch the expert.

Summary

Here are the movements that I did with Mark. Try them out at your own speed, so that you can learn from yourself.

1. First, stand still at the side of the trail. Begin to shift your weight from left to right so that you lift each ski a little off the snow as you place your weight on the other ski. Feel how the pressure on the sole of each foot increases and decreases as you shift. Scan your body with your attention and feel what you are doing to cause the pressure to shift from one foot to the other and back. Notice your breathing. Is it smooth and easy? When the movement feels easy, try it while skiing slowly back and forth across the trail. (Fig 4–1A/B)

Fig 4–1A   Fig 4–1B

2. Now, repeat the movements from the second lesson of shifting your weight in such a way that the point of maximum pressure shifts from side to side across your feet, and the skis tilt left and right. (Fig 4–2A/B)

Fig 4–2A   Fig 4–2B

3. Feel what you must do with your body to perform the two previous movements. What is the exact difference? In each movement there is a shift from side to side. In one movement, your total weight shifts from one ski to the other and back. In the other movement, you have approximately half of your weight on each ski, and your weight shifts from left to right across the soles of your feet so that the skis tilt from side to side. Being able to make fine distinctions like this is one of the keys to high-level skiing. If you don't figure out the difference right away, let go of the problem for a few days, and then try it again. As your awareness increases, you will be able to feel the exact difference between the two movements.

5

John: Feeling the World

John was a fairly good skier, somewhere in the high intermediate range. We had worked together a few times before, and he liked my awareness approach to ski instruction.

John liked to read a lot, and he read every ski technique book he could get his hands on, plus all of the national ski magazines. We used to have long discussions about how to ski, and how to learn to ski. He knew more about ski instruction than a lot of ski instructors.

One day we were discussing Tim Gallwey's *Inner Skiing.* I told John I liked the tone and overall approach of the book, but from my standpoint it could use a lot more technology.

John partly agreed with me, but said he liked the book and got a lot of good ideas from it. "You just say that it needs technology because you're an engineer and want everything spelled out to ten decimal places."

"Maybe you're right," I countered, "but all the computers I worked on are still running."

"But there is one thing that I have never been able to get," John admitted. "There is a place in the book where he talks about a racing coach who claims that he can feel every inch of his skis. I don't believe that's possible. After all, you don't have any nerve endings in your skis. How can you feel something if there aren't any nerves there?"

"Have you ever heard of something called Tactile Sensory Replacement?" I asked John.

"What? No. What's that got to do with skiing?"

"Tactile Sensory Replacement, or TSR as it's sometimes called, is a means of getting blind people to 'see' by replacing vision with a sensation on the skin," I said. "They have a device where a TV camera is mounted on the head, and then the TV picture is translated into a pattern of pressure on the skin of the back. After a period of training, blind people can get around pretty well by using one. They can learn to interpret the patterns of pressure on their back as being objects out in front of themselves. Neurophysiologists call that 'projection.' We all do that when we see. We interpret the patterns of light on the retina of the eye as being objects outside of ourselves.

"Also, neurophysiologists have been able to produce what you might call a kinesthetic illusion, and to fool people into feeling a physical sensation of touch in the empty air. It's supposed to be an eerie feeling.

"So if blind people can learn to 'feel' what's out in front of them without touching, and other people can feel a touch in thin air, it shouldn't be so difficult to feel your skis, right?"

"I see what you mean," John replied, "but I've tried a lot of times to feel what's happening in my skis and I've never felt anything different."

"I'll bet you just ski along and try to feel, right?" I asked.

"Yeah, that's pretty much what I do," John replied.

"That's your problem," I told John. "When you're skiing and turning in your usual way, you are locked into your habitual patterns of moving and sensing. It's very difficult to change those patterns *while you are in them.* That's why I had you ski very slowly across the trail when we worked before. And that's what you have to do if you want to learn to feel your skis."

"Have you got a lesson for that?" he asked me.

"You bet," I said.

"How about the bottom of the B lift tomorrow at ten?"

"You're on," I said.

I met John the next day and we rode up the lift. At the top I found a flat section.

"Stand here," I told John, indicating the flat section. "Now, just lift one ski up and set it down *very* slowly on the snow. Take at least sixty seconds to put your full weight on the ski."

I watched for while as John lifted and lowered his right ski a number of times.

"This is really something," he said, after a few minutes. "I can feel all sorts of things I never felt before. I can feel the tip and the tail touch, and then the ski begins to flex and there is a very gradual increase of pressure on the sole of my foot. Then the middle of the ski touches the snow and the pressure increases much faster."

"Close your eyes and just sense each foot and ski, and tell me what you feel," I said.

"The right foot feels more alive than the left one. It's like it's been sensitized somehow."

"Great," I said. "Now you're ready for part two. Here's what I want you to do. Ski very slowly across the trail, like you did when we worked before. Start with your right ski down hill. While you're skiing, lean forward so that your weight is on the ball of your foot, and tilt the right ski a little down hill so that you decrease the edge angle."

John began to do what I had said. Because he had his weight forward as he tilted the right ski downhill, the tip of the ski began to slideslip down the hill a little, making a scraping noise.

"Let the tip of the ski slide a little like that, then bring it back close to the tip of the uphill ski, then let it slide down again, and so on," I said. "Now the trick is, you have to *watch* the ski tip, *listen* to that scraping noise, and *feel* the vibrations that the scraping causes in the ski, all at the same time."

"What's that going to accomplish?" John asked.

"By doing that you engage the three major sensory input channels—visual, auditory, and kinesthetic—all at once. After a while, your nervous system will assemble the sensations in a new way and you will be able feel the vibration of the ski as originating up near the tip. Or, to put it a different way, you will be able to 'feel the ski,' even though you don't have any nerve endings there."

John began to ski slowly across the trail, concentrating on his skis. When he reached the side, I asked him to turn around and ski normally back across the trail, and then to repeat the exercise using only the right ski. "That way, you will be able to feel the difference in the legs and feet caused by the movements," I told him.

After a number of traverses John stopped and said, "I'm starting to feel what you mean. It sure is a weird feeling."

"Good," I told him. "Now try it while leaning backward, and letting the tail of the ski slide down the hill. That way, you can learn to feel the tail in the same way. Only this time, don't look at the ski. Just listen and feel."

After some more traverses John stopped and said, "You know, my right side and my left side are starting to feel like they belong to two different people."

"Yeah," I said, "When you change the way you perceive the world like this, you also change the way you perceive yourself. Make a few turns and tell me what you feel."

John started skiing and made about three turns, then stopped. "Man," he said, "my left leg feels like a piece of wood compared to my right. My right ski feels different from the left, too."

"Go back through the whole movement sequence again, but on the left side," I told him. "That way you can balance yourself out. You also might try repeating some of the movements later on in the week, until they really sink in."

As I started down the hill, I saw John slowly lifting and lowering his left ski. Nobody likes to feel unbalanced like that for long, even though it's a very useful learning experience.

About a week later I was finishing a cup of coffee before the lifts opened when John came up to my table and sat down. "I had the strangest experience," he said. "It was about three days after we did the exercise, on Thursday, the powder day."

I remembered that the previous Thursday we had about a foot of fine, Rocky Mountain powder. It had been one of the best days of the year, so far.

"So what happened?" I asked.

"Well, it was in the middle of the afternoon. All the powder had been skied off the trails, so I was dodging into the trees to

51

get some more powder there. I was skiing along, and then I guess the tip of my left ski hit something under the snow. It felt like a small branch. I felt it hit the tip of my ski, and then slide all the way down the length of the ski to the tail. I could even feel how it slid from side to side on the ski. The sensation was just as clear as if the branch had scraped along the sole of my foot. It was as if I had suddenly grown nerve endings into my ski."

"That's what you wanted, right?" I asked.

"Yeah, but I got a little more than that," John said. "The feeling surprised me so much that I completely forgot I was skiing. I fell into a tree well and it took me a half hour to dig out." He looked at me accusingly. "But I guess it was worth it."

Summary

Here's what I did with John to help him learn to feel his skis.

1. First, stand still on a flat spot on the snow. Lift your right ski up completely off the snow, and then *very* slowly set it back down, placing your full weight upon it. Take about 60 seconds to put the ski all the way down. As you set the ski down, pay careful attention to the sensations in your foot. Notice how the two ends of the ski touch the snow, and then how the ski begins to flex as the pressure increases. Can you feel the exact point where the whole ski is flat on the snow? Repeat the movement a number of times. Does the tip of the ski touch the snow first, or is it the tail? Try both ways. Can you feel whether the tip or the tail touch the snow first without looking at the ski? (Fig 5–1)

Fig 5–1

2. Find a wide, flat beginner or easy intermediate-level slope. Begin to ski slowly across the slope with your right side down hill. Lean forward a little, and begin to tilt the right ski left and right. As you tilt the ski to the right, so that the down-hill edge drops down, the tip of the right ski will slide downhill away from the tip of the left ski. Let the tip slide down a few inches, then bring the tips of the skis together, then let the right ski slide again, and so on. As the tip of the right ski slides downhill, it will make a scraping noise on the snow. Watch the tip of the ski, listen to the scraping sound, and feel the vibrations

Fig 5–2

of the ski tip with your foot. When you get to the side of the trail, stop, turn around, go back to the other side, and then repeat the exercise still using the right foot. After a while, you should be able to feel the vibrations of the ski as originating up near the tip of the ski. (Fig 5–2)

3. Continue to ski slowly across the trail, but now lean back a little. Again tilt the right ski left and right a little so that the tail of the right ski slides downhill away from the tail of the left ski. This time, just lis-ten to the scraping noise caused by the ski sliding across the snow, and feel the vibra-tions with your right foot. (Fig 5–3)

Fig 5–3

4. Close your eyes and pick up your right ski and shake it around gently a little in the air. Try the same thing with your left ski. What difference do you feel between the two legs? Which leg feels bigger? Which feels lighter? Make a few easy turns and compare the feeling in your legs while skiing. Which leg works better? Can you feel the ski and the snow better with one foot?

5. Go back through the whole sequence of moves with your left leg and improve that one too. After you are finished, make a few easy turns and pay close attention to the sensations in your feet. Can you feel the skis go over the small bumps and depressions in the snow as you ski?

6

Kay: Action and Intention

Kay was another of my early students. At the time I worked with her I was still experimenting with people, and I didn't know what to expect from the lessons I gave them. My guiding idea was that if a person could learn to feel how all the parts of their body moved on skis, and how the use of one part affected the others, they would improve.

Kay had been skiing for about five years and was an intermediate skier. She was fairly relaxed on skis and did a stem turn easily on beginner and intermediate slopes. She absolutely refused to attempt any slope marked Most Difficult.

Kay was one of the most cautious skiers I had ever seen. She rarely went more than about ten miles an hour on skis. I knew that Kay needed to speed up a little to improve her skiing, but I was fairly sure that just telling her to go faster wouldn't do the trick.

Kay had a girlfriend who was her exact opposite in temperament. Her girlfriend, Mara, had only been skiing for three years, but she was considerably better than Kay. Mara attacked every hill with great force. She ate a lot of snow, but that didn't seem to bother her a bit, and she improved rapidly.

I was skiing with Mara and Kay one day when Mara decided she was going to force Kay to get on an expert trail and just "do it."

"I know if I can just get her moving that she'll be able to handle it," Mara told me. "She's better than she knows, she just needs a little push."

I wasn't so sure that this was a good idea, but Mara insisted, and so I kind of went along for the ride.

We went up to the very top of the mountain, to an area that Kay didn't know, and then went down a long catwalk to the head of a small valley. From there on, all of the trails were designated Most Difficult, and Kay either had to walk all the way back up that long catwalk, or ski the expert terrain. It was a dirty trick, for sure, but Mara was Kay's best friend, and she insisted that she knew what she was doing.

The descent turned out to be a hellish experience. As soon as Kay saw the expert slope she stiffened up like a house cat being forced into a bath. She lost all control and plowed into a snowbank and fell. When she managed to get out, covered with snow from head to foot, she was furious.

Both Mara and I saw right away that this wasn't going to work, and so we just coached Kay slowly down the hill, a little at a time. It took us an hour to get Kay down a slope that most good skiers would ski in ten or fifteen minutes.

Later on that evening, Mara bought Kay a few drinks and got her to laugh about her experience. After all, the only thing that was really hurt was her ego.

It was painfully obvious that Mara's 'go for broke' method of learning, which worked so well for her, wouldn't do the job for Kay.

But what would? Kay was interested in improving and took lessons at the ski school on a fairly regular basis, but she felt that she hadn't improved much in the last year or two.

So Kay decided—after making me swear on a stack of Bibles that I wouldn't repeat Mara's trick—to try some of my awareness exercises.

I spent several days working with Kay's feet, having her lean forward and back, left and right, and so on, all the while feeling how the pressure shifted on the soles of her feet.

Kay loosened up a little, and she looked more solid on her skis somehow, but she still did her slow, cautious stem turn all the time.

On the fourth day I started doing turning exercises with Kay. I had noticed that she always kept her hips, her shoulders, and her head pointing in the same direction as her skis, and I guessed she didn't feel that these parts could turn independently of each other while on skis.

On the way up the lift I asked Kay to sit facing straight up the lift line. "Look down at your feet and skis," I asked Kay, "and tell me what you see."

Kay straightened up in her seat and looked down at her skis. "What am I looking for?" she asked.

"Notice the angle that each ski makes with the lift cable," I said. "Or, notice how far each ski turns out to the side, which amounts to the same thing."

"The left one turns out a lot further than the right," she said. "What does that mean?"

"It means you're unbalanced," I said.

"Oh, thanks. That's just what I need to hear at nine in the morning. Couldn't you at least wait till I've had my coffee?"

"That difference in the way you hold your skis will translate into a difference in the way you turn to one side or the other," I pointed out.

"I do turn more easily to one side," Kay said. "Is that the cause of it?"

"Yeah, that's the cause, but the root of it is higher up in your body. That's what we are going to work on today."

To begin, I had Kay stand still at the side of the trail and set her poles down beside her. Then I had her turn left and right.

"As you turn from side to side, just scan your body with your attention," I told her. "Make sure you can feel that your hips are turning over your feet, your shoulders are turning over your hips, and your head and eyes are turning also, so that you look all the way to one side and then the other."

I gave Kay a few minutes to get the feel of the motion, then I said, "Turn all the way to the left and stop, and measure your turning angle by noticing how far you can see to the side. Then do the same thing to the right." Kay could turn about a hundred or a hundred and ten degrees to the left, but slightly less than that to the right.

I pointed out the difference to her. "That imbalance in the way that you turn to each side has to do with one foot turning out further than the other, and it makes it easier for you to turn to one side than the other."

"So am I stuck like that?" Kay asked.

"Not for long," I replied.

"Turn back all the way to the left and stop," I directed Kay. "Now, hold your body still, and just turn your head and eyes to the right and look to the right, and then turn back to the left and look to the left, and so on, about fifteen or twenty times.

"OK. Now, turn everything left and right a few times . . . and then turn to the left and stop. Now just move your eyes and look left and right about twenty times, and make sure you breathe."

Then I asked Kay to turn left and right a few more times, and finally to stop when she was all the way to the left.

"Measure your turning angle now," I told Kay.

Her eyebrows shot up. "Wow. I can look almost all the way behind me now. If feels like I've almost doubled my turning angle."

"Great," I said. "Now let's do the other side." I watched as Kay repeated the movements of her head and eyes while turned to the right.

I said to Kay, "Now the trick is to be able to do that twisting movement while you're sliding along the snow. So, try it while you are skiing very slowly across the hill."

Kay began to ski slowly across the hill and to turn her whole body—hips, shoulders, head, and eyes—to the left and right. It took her a few traverses to start to feel comfortable with the movement, and once or twice she lost her balance and fell. But, since she was only going about three or four miles an hour, they were easy falls, and she didn't mind them.

As I watched Kay I could see that the twisting movement was becoming easy and fluid. At first she had held her breath, but now she was breathing easily and appeared to be relaxed and at ease.

"Keep turning just like you're doing and measure your turning angle," I told Kay.

She turned a few times and then stopped. "I'm not turning as far as I was when I was standing still," she told me. "What causes that?"

"You stiffen yourself up when you start to move, like just about every other skier on the hill, and you don't feel it. Try it standing still again, and then start off very slowly, and make sure you don't tense yourself up when you start moving. If you start out very slowly and pay careful attention to yourself, you will be able to feel it when you start to stiffen yourself up. When you can feel it, it's not so hard to let go of it."

I watched Kay twist left and right a few times, and then very slowly start off on the traverse. She stopped and started several times.

Then she beckoned me to come over to her. "It feels like I'm pulling my head down and my shoulders up a little. Is that what you mean?"

"That's what it looks like to me," I said. "Can you start off without doing that?"

"I think so, let me see."

Kay began to ski again, slowly. I didn't see her pull her head down this time. We were almost at the bottom. I skied over to the lift and Kay joined me. We got on and started up.

"Watch the skiers, I want to show you something," I said to Kay. We were in an area of mostly beginner and intermediate trails, and most of the skiers were intermediates.

"See how that man in the blue suit skis," I said pointing. He turns his whole body and his skis left and right as a unit, as if they were one piece. He doesn't feel that he can do the twisting movement you just did. That's what makes him look so awkward."

I pointed out several other skiers who were doing the same thing.

Suddenly Kay said, "I see what you're talking about. It looks like everybody on the hill is doing it. Have you seen anybody who *isn't* skiing like that?" she asked.

"Not so far," I said, "but we will. The thing I want you to notice is how practically all beginner and intermediate-level skiers lock themselves up like that. In fact, I think that the inability to turn the body and skis independently of each other is the single biggest factor which separates the intermediates from the advanced skiers. If you don't feel that your body and skis can turn independently of each other, a parallel turn is just about impossible."

I had been watching the trail as I spoke, and suddenly I saw a good skier come over a headwall and ski down right under us. It was a perfect vantage point.

"Watch that man," I said to Kay, "and tell me what you see."

"His body and skis are turning independently of each other, all right. He sure looks a lot better than those other people we were watching."

At the top, we got off and skied over to the trail.

"Try that twisting movement some more," I said. I want to make sure that you really have it cold."

Kay started slowly across the trail, twisting her body left and right.

As Kay was doing the movements, I managed to get about fifty yards downhill from her. We were on a moderately steep section of an intermediate slope. She stopped and said something to me, but I couldn't hear her. "Come down here," I yelled up, "I can't hear you."

Kay pointed her skis down the fall line, and made about five perfect parallel turns as she skied down to me. She looked like she was ready for the Olympics. She did a perfect stop right beside me.

I had skied a lot with Kay, and I knew her style well. The change in her skiing was so great that for a second I thought that someone else had taken her place on the hill while I wasn't looking. I peered carefully at the figure standing beside me just to be sure. It was Kay, all right.

Her eyes were wide. "What was *that?*" she asked.

"*That,*" I told her, "is what you have been trying to do for the last few years. Some people call it a parallel turn."

"Do it again," I told Kay. She started to ski again, but went back to her old stem turn. "I can't do it," she said, after several tries.

I insisted that if she had done it once, she could do it again, but the harder she tried, the more she became locked into her old turn. Finally I saw that she wasn't going to be able to repeat her improved performance, and I quit insisting. I was disappointed, and so was Kay. I began to think that her breakthrough had been some kind of a fluke, and didn't really mean anything. I had completely forgotten that the same thing happened to me when I had my first big breakthrough.

We finished the day and drove home. I thought about what happened to Kay off and on for a few weeks, but I couldn't decide what to make of it.

Then one day I got a phone call. It was Kay. "I got my turn back," she said excitedly. "I can do it almost every time now."

I asked her what happened, and Kay told me an interesting story.

She had gone skiing several times after our last lesson, and each time she tried to repeat her parallel turn, but she had not succeeded even once. Finally she just gave up altogether and decided to enjoy herself, but she did practice the twisting movement I had shown her a few times. Right after that she did another series of perfect parallel turns, but this second time it wasn't such a big surprise, and she managed to feel what she was doing. She noticed that the new turn felt almost effortless compared with her old stem turn.

She experimented a little and found that when she "tried to turn," as she put it, she would do her old stem turn. However, when she "just sort of quit trying and let go," she would do the new parallel turn.

By the end of the day, she was doing the new turn all the time. And, she said, "I feel like a new woman on skis. It's incredible.

"Oh, there's one other thing. Remember how my skis turned out at different angles when I sat on the lift? Now they're almost equal."

I thanked Kay for sharing her experience with me, and hung up the phone. I thought about what she had told me, but at first I couldn't make any sense out of it. When she tried to do it, she couldn't, and when she didn't try, she could.

As I taught more people, I found that Kay's experience was fairly common. A student would have a big breakthrough, and then be unable to repeat it. Later on, the new way—whatever it happened to be—would come back, and after a while it would become their new habitual way of skiing.

I had to do a lot of thinking to figure out why Kay couldn't repeat her improved turn right away, and why she had to "quit trying and let go" to make it work.

When we learn a complicated physical act, such as a turn on skis, we begin by forming an intention to turn. We say to ourselves, "Now I am going to turn," and then we do whatever it is that we do to turn. As we learn, this sequence becomes unconscious and automatic, so that we "just turn."

Each person turns in his own individual way, whatever that may be, but the initial step in the turning sequence is the intention to turn. Once we decide to turn, the rest of the steps in the sequence follow automatically.

When Kay had her breakthrough, she wasn't thinking so hard about turning, and the new, improved turn had a chance to manifest itself. Right after that, she became so excited that she began "trying to turn," and that trying strongly activated her old sequence of movements, which was her stem turn. The harder she tried, the harder she pushed herself back into the old movement pattern.

Later on, when she gave up and quit trying, she took the power out of the initial step, which is the intention to turn, and the new, easier, better turn popped out again. After that it was just a matter of paying attention and practicing until Kay could do the new turn whenever she liked. She had managed to hook a new, improved movement sequence—a parallel turn instead of a stem turn—onto her intention to turn. My main contribution to all this was to give her the initial experience of feeling how her body could twist left and right over her skis. Once she could feel how her whole body was involved in this motion, which she had blocked out of her skiing movement repertory, the parallel turn was a snap.

Summary

Here's what I did to get Kay to feel how her body can turn left and right over her skis. As usual, choose a smooth, wide, easy slope to try this, and move slowly so that you can feel all the details of the movement.

1. Stand still at the side of the trail and set your poles down. Begin to turn your whole body left and right in an easy, twisting movement. As you twist, scan your body with your attention. Notice how your feet move, then your ankles, then your knees, then hips, shoulders, head, and eyes. Let yourself breathe easily as you twist. Scan your body from top to bottom several times. (Fig 6–1A/B)

Fig 6–1A   Fig 6–1B

2. Turn all the way to the left and stop. Measure your turning angle by mentally marking the spot where your eyes are looking. Then, turn all the way to the right and measure the turning angle there. (Fig 6–2)

Fig 6–2

3. Turn your whole body left and right a few times and then turn to the left and stop. Keeping your whole body still, turn just your head and eyes left and right, so that you turn your head to each side and look to that side about twenty times. (Fig 6–3A/B)

Fig 6–3A

Fig 6–3B

4. Then, turn your whole body left and right a few times, and again stop when you are turned all the way to the left. Keep your whole body still, and moving only your eyes, look left

and right about twenty times. Be sure to breathe while you are doing all of this. (Fig 6–4A/B)

Fig 6–4A

Fig 6–4B

5. Turn your whole body left and right a few more times and stop while looking to the left. Measure your turning angle now.

How much has it increased? The improvement in the turning angle is the result of the relaxation of the muscles in the body caused by moving the torso, head, and eyes independently of each other. (Fig 6–5)

Repeat the movements of the head and eyes twisting to the right and improve that side also.

6. Now, pick up your poles and begin to ski slowly across the trail. As you ski, begin to twist

Fig 6–5

your whole body left and right. Start with a small twist, and gradually increase the turning angle. When you get to the side of the trail, stop, turn around, and ski back the other way. As you move, slowly scan your body with your attention. Let yourself breathe easily, and make sure that each part of your body is turning. You should be able to feel that your hips are turning over your feet, your shoulders are turning over your hips, your head is turning over your shoulders, and your eyes are turning in your head. Spend as much time as you need with this movement until it feels easy and comfortable. Notice if you turn as far to each side while moving as you did while standing still. (Fig 6–6A/B)

Fig 6–6A   Fig 6–6B

7. Make a few turns on an easy slope and notice how your skiing feels. Do you allow your skis to turn independently of your body, or do you keep all the parts stuck together?

7

Kim:
Independent Leg Action

Riding up on the lift for a lesson with Kim and talking about skiing, I found out that she had started when she was very young, and had skied a lot. I could tell that she was a very good skier just from listening to her descriptions of some of the places she had skied.

So when we got off the lift at the top, I decided I would ask Kim to ski on a fairly difficult slope so I could evaluate her skiing. Under pressure from bumps and steeps, any small faults in a skier's technique become magnified. I figured if I watched Kim ski on a groomed intermediate slope, that she, being an advanced skier, would exhibit near-perfect form, and I would have a difficult time finding something to work on. As it turned out, something entirely different from what I expected happened, and I gave one of my most interesting lessons ever.

Going straight back down the lift line was a moderately steep bump trail. The trail hadn't been groomed in a few weeks, and the bumps were pretty big, although not quite up to the "killer mogul" stage. There was about a hundred yards of easy, groomed slope leading to the bump trail.

"Let's do that one," I said to Kim, pointing to the bump trail, "I want to watch you ski."

Kim took off down the hill, and I watched carefully. She looked great on her skis. Her motions were smooth and flowing, and all the parts of her body seemed to be working easily to make each turn.

However, she was turning in a peculiar way, at least according to my way of thinking. She was using a technique skiers call "independent leg action."

This "independent leg action" turn is characterized by an initial, unnecessary move made by the uphill foot at the beginning of the turn. To do this turn, the uphill foot is lifted off the snow, and moved a few inches away from the downhill foot in such a way that the tail of the uphill ski moves further than the tip. After this, the turn is completed in the usual way.

About a decade ago, this kind of turn was being taught to recreational skiers as the best way to turn.

I continued to watch Kim as she headed into the bumps. She reached the edge of the bumps, and she continued to move her legs apart and together as she turned in the bumps. My eyebrows shot up to my hairline. I couldn't believe what I was seeing. Kim was trying to use her independent leg action turn in the bumps!

Kim managed to go through about four or five turns before she lost it. However, she didn't just stiffen up and fall, as many skiers would do, but instead turned her skis across the fall line and stopped. She had good balance and control, that was for sure.

I skied up to Kim and stopped. She started to say something about how she had always had trouble in the bumps, but I interrupted her. "Why are you using that independent leg action when you turn?" I asked her. "Have you been taking lessons with a regular ski instructor?"

Her reaction to my outburst was strange, to say the least. She bent forward at her hips, and remained there, supported in that position by her hands on her poles. For a few seconds I couldn't figure out what she was doing, but then I saw her body shaking, and I realized she was laughing.

She stood up, still laughing. "How did you know that?" she asked. "I mean, I *am* a ski instructor, or at least I used to be one, a couple of years ago when I lived in Utah."

I couldn't answer Kim's question right away, my mind was racing along on a different track. I thought that I had a chance to give Kim a dramatic lesson, and I was trying to figure out the best way to proceed. I could see that she already had most of the skills she needed to be a really good skier. Her movements were fluid, and she used her whole body to make each turn. Her use of her body as she skied was excellent.

Kim had a different problem from most of my other students. She had fallen into the trap of the independent leg action turn, as I call it. It was an easy trap to fall into, unfortunately, since at that time this kind of turn was being widely promoted as "The Modern Way to Ski." However, this kind of turn is modern only in the sense that tail fins on automobiles were modern some years back. I expect that like the wide track turn, which was also "The Modern Way to Ski" not so long ago, the independent leg action turn will also fade away. In the meantime, though, it has caused recreational skiers a lot of trouble.

There is, however, one place where this turn is useful. It is the turn that most racers use when running a race course. In the artificial situation of racing, where the skier is forcing himself to turn as fast as he possibly can around a series of poles placed in the snow, this is the turn of choice. This constitutes much of the appeal of this turn, as well, since "this is the way the racers ski." Outside of the racing situation, however, this turn is not very useful. And in the bumps, the initial movement of the uphill foot destroys the rhythm of the bumps, and makes turning very difficult, if not impossible.

Of course, this turn is not "wrong," and many good skiers will spontaneously use it on occasion, especially if forced into a situation where they must make a very sharp turn at high speed. However, from the standpoint of *learning* to ski, this kind of turn causes a tremendous problem. Initiating the turn with a foot movement causes the student to focus even more of his attention on his feet, when it should be directed to his whole body.

Most of the skiers I work with don't feel what they are doing. They feel they are bending their knees when they are not, or that their torso is vertical when it is pitched forward 45-degrees, and so on. Much of my teaching with these skiers is devoted to getting them to feel what they are actually doing. Kim, however, had a good feeling for what she was doing, but she was trying to do the wrong thing. The kind of problem Kim had usually comes from analyzing and thinking about skiing, rather than just feeling the easiest way to ski.

I knew that if I could break Kim out of her habit of separating her feet at the beginning of each turn, I could improve her skiing dramatically. I thought I knew what would work. I looked at Kim and remembered she had asked me a question. "I said, 'How did you know I was a ski instructor?'" Kim repeated. I realized I had been thinking about what to do with Kim for over a minute, and had forgotten where I was.

"Just about the only people I see skiing like that outside a race course are ski instructors," I told her.

Kim began to explain the rationale of independent leg action, but I interrupted her. "Would you like to try something different?" I asked her.

"Sure," she said, "why not?"

We got off the bump trail and onto a groomed intermediate slope. This terrain was well within Kim's level of ability, and I knew she would be able to direct all her attention to learning, and not have to worry about falling.

I had her stand on a flat spot at the side of the trail and turn her whole body, and head and eyes, left and right. When she could do this easily, I had her measure the turning angle to each side. She could turn about a hundred degrees to each side.

Then I had her turn to the side and stop, and from that position turn her head and eyes in different combinations of movements. After about fifteen minutes of this, her turning angle had increased to just over 180 degrees each way.

At this point I usually ask the student to repeat the turning movements while skiing slowly across the trail, but with Kim I figured I could skip some intermediate steps, and go straight to the main point.

"Do you remember that old dance called The Twist?" I asked her. I bent my knees and elbows and rotated my hips left and right while rotating my shoulders and arms in the opposite direction a few times to show her what I was talking about.

"Sure," she told me, "Wasn't it popular back in the 1950s?"

"That's the one," I said. "What I would like for you to do is to make that movement while skiing slowly across the slope."

Kim began to ski slowly back and forth across the slope while doing The Twist. She had never tried a move like that on skis before, so at first she was a little hesitant. After three or four traverses, however, she began to feel comfortable and to loosen up a bit, and I saw that the motion of her upper body began to go down to her skis.

"Notice that when you make that movement with your upper body," I told her, "the motion goes down to your feet and turns your skis. Just continue to do that, and exaggerate the part of the movement where your downhill shoulder moves backward, and your downhill hip moves forward, and notice what that does to your skis. The easiest way to do it is to just pull your down hill elbow backward with a quick, snappy movement."

After a few more traverses Kim could feel that when she did that movement, the tips of her skis turned up the hill a little.

"It helps if I bend my knees a little bit as I turn," she said.

"That's right," I told her. "Now do the same thing, but move a little faster."

Kim began to experiment with the movement, while I watched expectantly. I could tell from the absorbed look on her face that something was going on. Kim's posture began to change as she worked with the movement, and suddenly she began to feel that if her weight were balanced just right, she could do the movement and turn her skis across her line of motion and stop. This move is usually called a hockey stop by skiers.

I could see that Kim was really getting into it. She was going faster and faster just to see how quickly she could stop. Although she was going from a fairly high speed to a complete stop in just a few feet, and throwing up a big cloud of snow in the process, the move appeared easy and elegant.

Kim stopped and pulled up her goggles. "Wow," she said, "that's incredible. I've never felt anything like that on skis before. It feels like there's a giant spring inside holding me up. What causes that, anyway?"

"That 'spring' feeling comes from two different factors," I told Kim. "When you did that twisting movement standing still, it lengthened the muscles along your spine. That allowed you to rotate further, of course, but it also freed the spine to act as a natural shock absorber. If the muscles are tight along the spine, the 'spring' is already compressed and can't rebound like it should. The other factor was the movement like The Twist. That was actually kind of a trick to get you to turn your skis without separating them.

"When you use that independent leg action and separate your feet, all the weight of your body has to come up one leg, at an angle, and it's a real strain to hold yourself up. You almost have to stiffen your body. When your feet are together, your weight comes straight up both legs, like it should, and it is a lot easier to hold yourself up. In fact, there is a reflex in the body that does that, and when you get it just right, it almost feels like there's a wire from overhead holding you up.

"Try the same thing in those bumps over there," I said, pointing to some small moguls at the side of the trail.

Kim skied over to the little bumps and began doing the stopping movement by rotating her hips and shoulders in opposite directions. At first the bumps interfered with the rotation, but soon she figured out how to time the movement so that it synchronized with the bumps.

"That looks great," I told Kim. "Now, try the same thing, but this time don't stop. Just slow down a little."

This was the payoff movement. If everything went right, Kim would fall into a perfect bump technique. I knew she had the balance and the skill to do it. The only thing that would stop her would be reverting to her old "independent leg action." I was counting on the new sensations she had been experiencing to help her break through into the new movement.

Kim started down through the little bumps. She began too fast and lost her rhythm and stopped. I started to tell her to slow down, but as I watched she took a deep breath and began to ski again, much more slowly. She made a half-dozen slow, hesitant turns, and then suddenly her body caught the rhythm and she flashed quickly down to the end of the bump field.

"Wow," she said. "So *that's* how they do it. All I had to do was get my upper body involved in the turn."

I started to congratulate Kim, but suddenly she turned and plunged into the trees at the side of the trail.

"Come on," she said. I realized she was cutting through the short stand of trees to get back to the big bumps on the trail where we started the lesson.

I wanted her to do some more practice on the little bumps before getting into the biggies, but she was long gone. All I could do was follow through the trees.

When I got to the bump trail, Kim was nowhere to be seen. Then I looked downhill and saw her head and shoulders disappearing over a headwall. "So much for my idea that she needs some more practice," I said to myself.

I took off and caught up with Kim in the lift line. She was grinning from ear to ear. "I've always wanted to do that," she said. "Bumps have always been the sore spot in my skiing. But I've got it now."

Summary

Here's a summary of the exercise I did with Kim to help her learn to feel how the movements of her upper body turn the skis. Before you start these movements, briefly review the turning movements from the previous lesson, number six. Notice how in that lesson you skied slowly across the slope while turning all the parts of your body left and right together. In this lesson you will be able to improve even more by learning to turn different parts of your body—in this case, the hips and shoulders—in opposite directions.

1. As usual, pick a wide, flat, beginner or easy intermediate-level slope. Go to the side of the trail and stand still, setting your poles on the snow. Bend your knees and your elbows, so your arms are in the position you would use to run or ski.

   Begin to rotate your hips and shoulders in opposite directions, as in the Fifties dance called The Twist. Make the movements slow, light, and easy, so you can feel what you are doing. As you move, scan your body with your attention. Let your awareness move from your feet to your head and back, many times. Pay particular attention to the movements of your hips and shoulders. (Fig 7–1A/B)

Fig 7–1A   Fig 7–1B

Many people, when they first try this movement, rotate their hips and shoulders in the same direction even though they *feel* as if they are rotating them in opposite directions. Others do not rotate their hips at all, but instead move their pelvis from side to side, or tilt their pelvis so that first one hip is higher, then the other.

As you do the movement, look at your body from time to time and compare what you feel with what you see. If the movement continues to give you trouble or seems unclear, ask a friend to watch you and tell you what he sees, or try the movement at home in front of a full-length mirror. Surprisingly, many people require quite a bit of practice with attention before this simple movement becomes clear in their awareness.

2. Now, pick up your poles and begin to ski slowly across the slope. Continue to rotate your hips and shoulders in opposite directions. Make a number of slow traverses while scanning

74

your body with your attention until the movement feels easy and fluid. (Fig 7–2A/B)

Fig 7–2A

Fig 7–2B

3. Continue to ski slowly across the slope while rotating your hips and shoulders in opposite directions, but now exaggerate one half of the movement: When you rotate your downhill shoulder backward, make it a quick, snapping movement. Think about pulling your downhill elbow backward very quickly. As you do this, of course, the uphill shoulder and arm will move forward. Continue this movement while scanning your body to make sure you do not stiffen up any part unnecessarily or hold your breath. (Fig 7–3)

After a few traverses, you should be able to feel that as you pull your downhill elbow back, rotating your shoulders around to face more down the

Fig 7–3

hill, your hips and skis will rotate in the opposite direction, so that the tips of the skis turn up the hill a little, and you come to a stop. Make sure you don't stiffen your knees as you rotate your hips and shoulders. As the motion becomes easy, speed up a little. You will find that you can stop very quickly like this. Is the movement equally easy on both sides? If the stopping movement is easy on one side and difficult on the other, can you feel what parts of your body are not helping with the movement on the difficult side, and so equalize the two sides?

8

May: A Total Change

She started with her fear. It had been festering inside her for almost twenty years, limiting her ability to be who she wanted to be, and to do what she wanted to do. She had given up skiing because of it and, I suspect, many other things. Her name was May, and one day our paths crossed.

May did a lot of skiing in grade school, but then gave it up. Now, at age 38, she had decided to get back into it. She told me her biggest problem was a fear of falling and injuring herself. For the past 20 years the most athletic endeavor she attempted was an occasional jog of a half-mile or so. She feared she was out of shape, and possibly too old to learn to ski again. She wanted to know what I thought.

I told May that if she wanted to get back into skiing, she could probably do it. She was worried she had "forgotten everything," but I knew that like the skill of bicycle riding, you never really forget your skiing skills. It's possible to learn to ride a bike, then not get on one for years, and then to ride easily with just a few minute's practice.

Out on the hill we met several times and I worked with May, getting her to feel the bottoms of her feet, to note how her body could turn over her skis, and so on. She seemed particularly fearful of falling and kept her speed down to just a few miles per hour. I thought the lessons were going slowly, but I recognize that everyone learns at their own speed, and I didn't push May.

One evening we were talking about skiing, and I mentioned that I thought May could probably ski a little faster. I just wanted to get her to start thinking about speed.

"I'm still worried that I'll hurt myself." She suddenly took a deep breath, screwed up her face, and said, "It's my left knee. I hurt it years ago skiing, and it's always been a little stiff. That's why I go so slow."

"Let's have a look at your knee," I said. "Go put on some shorts." May came back in a minute wearing shorts.

"Stand right here in front of me," I told her. I looked at May's legs and saw right away what the trouble was. The arch on her left foot was collapsed and the front of the leg was rotated inward, and her left knee had moved inward a little.

I pointed out the differences between her two legs to May. "I always felt there was a difference, but I could never figure out exactly what it was," she said. "Is that fixable?"

"It sure is. In fact, we're going to fix it right now, but first, I want to show you something. Can you see how when the arch collapses the foot tilts inward? When you put skis on your feet, your left ski will tend to dig in its inside edge. That will make you unstable on skis, especially when you are turning to the right, because that's when the left ski takes most of your weight. With your foot like that, your weight doesn't come down straight through your knee. That puts a strain on it and makes it hurt."

May wiggled her left foot around a little, tilting it left and right. "I see what you mean," she said. "But how do we fix it?"

"Well," I said, "there's a trick. Tilt your left foot left and right again and notice what you do to tilt the foot, or to move the arch up and down, which is the same thing."

May began to tilt her left foot left and right on the floor. After a minute she said, "I'm doing something with my leg."

"Right," I said. "You have to rotate your leg left and right to tilt the foot. And the muscles that do the rotation are located around your hip joint. So to fix the foot, we actually have to change something in your hip. In fact, I was going to do something like this with you anyway, because that left and right tilting movement of the foot is important to be able to edge your skis with power and precision. Most skiers hardly use that particular movement, or even know about it. At least, I've never seen it in a ski instruction manual.

"So let's go. As you stand there, turn your whole body left and right, and feel what your feet do." May began to turn left and right, and after a minute she said, "My feet tilt left and right as I turn. And the right one moves a lot easier than the left."

"Exactly right," I said. "So what we're going to do is work with the right foot and hip first, since that one moves more easily. Doing that will kind of 'prime' the left side for improvement."

I asked May to go back to turning left and right, and to exaggerate the movement of her right foot. As she turned to the right, she tilted the right foot to the right, shifting her weight to the outside edge and curling her toes, making the arch high.

As she turned to the left, she tilted the right foot to the left, shifting the weight to the inside edge and flattening the arch.

Then I had her do a series of movements to improve the way the right foot and hip work together. I had her turn all the way to the right and stop, and then tilt her right foot left and right on the floor. Then I had her turn all the way to the left and stop, and tilt the right foot left and right. Next I had her hold the right foot tilted all the way to the right, with the arch high, and to turn her body left and right with the foot held immobile. Finally, I had her hold her right foot tilted all the way to the left, with the arch flat, and to turn her whole body left and right.

"This is a workout," said May.

"Take a break and walk around a little," I told her.

May started to walk around. "My left and right legs feel like they belong to two different people," she remarked. "My left leg feels like it's made of wood. And on the right side, I think I can feel every thread of fiber in the carpet when I set my foot down."

"Just think about how that sensitivity in your foot will enhance your skiing," I told May.

"Yeah, but what about the other side? I thought the point of this whole thing was to fix my left knee."

"Right. It's time for that now. Stand here in front of me again and begin to turn your whole body left and right, just as you did before, but this time exaggerate the movement of the left foot."

As May turned I repeated the directions so that she could get her left leg working. At one point she stopped and said, "I can feel the restriction in my left leg. It's stuck to the inside and doesn't want to turn to the outside, so the arch can rise."

"Right," I said. "Just turn the leg gently left and right, and feel your foot and hip joint at the same time. And breathe."

May fiddled with her leg for a few seconds and then she said, "There, that's it," and let out a big sigh. I saw the leg start to move in a different way.

"Walk around some and feel your legs and feet now," I said.

"Boy, my left leg feels *really* peculiar. I guess it had been stuck for a long time."

"Well, I think that's it for now," I told May. "Tomorrow we'll work on the hill."

The next day I met May up on the mountain. We started to work with the twisting movement of the body and how it relates to the tilting movement of the feet.

May seemed particularly fearful today. I judged that it was because we were getting down to the root of her fears about falling and hurting herself, which were somehow lodged in her previously injured left knee. I asked her to repeat the movements we had done the previous evening, at first standing still, and then skiing very slowly across the hill.

When we began working on her left leg she slowed down to a crawl. I stepped back to get a look at May. The expression on her face suggested that someone had just told her she had incurable cancer and was going to die a painful death within a few months. Her movements suggested that she was about eighty years old instead of forty, and her voice was slow, hesitant, and fearful. She would make one single slow turn and then come to a complete stop and just stand still, her poles dangling in the air, until I told her to move again. "She must have a hell of a lot of negative emotional energy wrapped up in her knee," I thought to myself. I wondered what had happened to her when she injured it.

We finally got down to the lift and got on. May seemed so nervous and distracted that I was afraid she was going to drop her poles, so I showed her how I lifted one leg and shoved the pole handles under the leg so that I was sitting on the poles and they couldn't fall.

With great hesitancy May tried to lift her leg and get the poles under it. It took her three tries to get it, and I thought she might fall off the lift.

I wondered if I should keep working with May or let her go for a day or two. My guess was that she was getting down to the root of some issue of great importance to her, and that I should continue unless she asked to stop.

We got off the lift and skied over to the trail. I continued to direct May in the twisting exercises as if nothing were out of the ordinary. About halfway down I sensed that she had had enough, and I told her I was going to let her ski by herself for a while, and that I would hook up with her in the afternoon. My thought was that she had plenty of instruction and now needed some time to digest the new information.

I took off and went way over to the other side of the mountain to ski with some friends for a while. It was about two-thirty when I came back to the lift that May was skiing.

As I stepped up to the lift I glanced at the chalk board. Printed in large block letters was this message: "Jack Heggie—Meet May on the trail."

Something about the abruptness of the message alarmed me. The thought flashed through my mind that she had injured herself. But no, she wouldn't still be skiing if that were the case.

I jumped on the lift and waited impatiently for it to reach the top. I wondered what was going on.

I skied over to the top of the trail and began to look for May. She had a solid dark suit with a light colored diagonal stripe down the back that was easy to spot, and I saw her about halfway down the trail. I skied down and stopped a few feet in front of her. As she skied by, I yelled out, "What's up?"

To my great surprise she skied right past me, just a few feet away, as if she hadn't heard me.

I skied down and again stopped a little in front of May. As she skied by I again hailed her, but again she skied right by me as if I weren't there.

"What is this?" I said to myself. A third time I skied up in front of May, almost right in her path, but this time I kept my mouth shut and just watched as she skied by. The fearful expression was gone, and she had a determined look on her face. Her eyes seemed to be boring into the trail in front of her, and I could sense that she didn't see me. She seemed to be in some kind of trance.

I fell in behind May and watched her skiing. She was making very quick linked stem turns, and moving much faster than I had ever seen her go on skis before. Her stance looked rock-solid and suggested great assurance and authority.

I followed May all the way down to the lift and we skied up and got on. She lifted her leg and shoved her pole handles under her outside leg with a movement as deft and assured as a samurai warrior sheathing his sword after a successful battle.

I opened my mouth to say something, but May cut me off with a brusque gesture. She began to speak in a quiet but confident voice. She was staring straight ahead, and her chin was jutting out in an almost belligerent way. "There are two things that you have to know in order to ski," she began.

She continued to lecture me for about ten minutes on exactly what was required in order to ski well. She sounded so confident and sure of herself that all I could do was sit there and nod in agreement every few minutes. I was amazed. She seemed like a totally different person. I began to feel as if I were the student and she the teacher, so strong was her conviction.

When we got off at the top she stopped to put on her pole straps, said "I'll see you later," and took off.

I stood there dumbfounded. I had never seen anyone change

so much so quickly.

I spent the rest of the day cruising around on some easy trails, thinking about what had happened to May.

She had started with her fear, and now it was gone, vanquished. The fear had been blocking her for almost twenty years.

In spite of that, I knew that the fear had a positive function. The fear stopped her from going so fast that she would fall and injure her weakened left knee. Many of these fears that skiers confront, I believe, have a real basis and serve a useful purpose in life and in skiing.

But once the physical basis for the fear had been removed, once her leg was functioning correctly, May was free to improve, and she did, with a huge jump. She sensed, at an unconscious level, that she was now free, and the fear removed itself.

I knew that when this happens, the mind experiences strange, sometimes almost trance-like states. I had been there a few times myself.

Summary

Here are the movements I did with May to help her improve. Try these movements first at home, wearing shorts so you can watch your feet and compare what you feel with what you see. When the movements are clear, try them again out on the mountain.

1. Stand with your feet about shoulder-width apart, and begin to turn your body left and right. As you turn, direct your attention to your feet. Notice how your feet tilt left and right on the floor. As you turn to the left, your feet tilt in such a way that the pressure moves to the outside edge of the left foot, and to the inside edge of the right foot. As you turn to the right, the feet tilt in the other direction. If you were wearing skis on your feet, the skis would make the movement of edging as you turn. (Fig 8–1A/B)

Continue to turn, and notice if one foot moves more easily than the other. As we do the exercise, we will start by describing the movements of the right foot. If your left foot moves more easily than your right, however, start with your left foot.

Fig 8–1A   *Fig 8–1B*

2. Continue to turn left and right, and exaggerate the movement of the right foot a little. As you turn to the right, tilt the right foot even further to the right and curl your toes so the arch of the foot rises. Then as you turn to the left, tilt the right foot to the inside edge and lift your toes so the arch flattens out. Do this for several minutes, until the movement of the foot is easy and smooth. (Fig 8–2A/B)

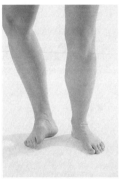
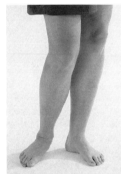

Fig 8–2A   *Fig 8–2B*

3. Now turn your body all the way to the right and stop. Holding your body still, tilt the right foot left and right about twenty times on the floor. Keep your right knee fairly straight but not locked. Notice what you do to tilt the right foot. You must rotate the right leg left and right at the hip joint to make this movement. (Fig 8–3A/B)

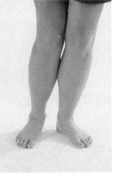
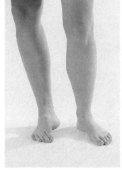

Fig 8–3A   *Fig 8–3B*

4. Turn your body left and right a few more times, and then stop with your body turned to the left. Holding your body still, tilt your right foot left and right another twenty times. Again, notice how the right leg moves to tilt the foot. (Fig 8–4A/B)

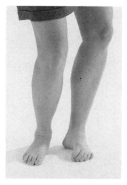 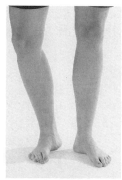

Fig 8–4A   *Fig 8–4B*

5. Turn your body left and right a few more times, and stop with your body turned to the right, the right foot tilted onto its right side with the arch high. Hold your right foot immobile in this position and turn your body left and right. Notice how holding the foot in this position inhibits the ability of the body to turn to the left. If the an-

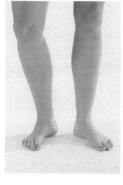 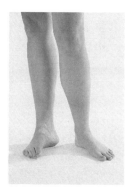

Fig 8–5A   *Fig 8–5B*

kle and hip do not work together easily, the hips lose their power and are unable to turn easily. Make about twenty turning movements, and then release the right foot and notice how much further you can turn to the left. (Fig 8–5A/B)

6. Turn your body left and right a few more times, and then stop with your body turned to the left and the right foot tilted to the left, so that the arch is flat and the pressure on the inside of the right foot. Hold your right foot immobile in this position and turn your body left and right. Notice how holding the foot in this position inhibits the ability of the body to turn to the right. (Fig 8–6A/B) Make another twenty easy turning move-

ments, and then release the right foot and let it tilt left and right as the body turns. Compare the feeling in the two feet now. Which moves more easily? Walk around a little and feel how each foot comes down onto the floor.

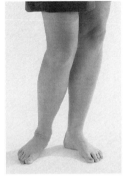 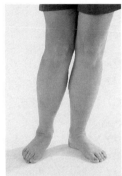

Fig 8–6A   *Fig 8–6B*

Take a few minute's break, and then repeat the exercise on the other side, and improve that one also.

7. The next time you go skiing, repeat all of these movements standing still on skis. Set your poles down and go through the whole exercise again, noticing how your skis tilt left and right as you turn. When you have finished, spend about ten or fifteen minutes skiing slowly back and forth across an easy slope and turning your body left and right. As you turn, just feel how your skis tilt a little left and right. When the movement feels easy and fluid, speed up a little and make a few turns. How does your improved awareness of how your hips and feet work together affect your skiing?

9

Lisa: The Balance Point for Turning

To be unbalanced is perhaps the greatest problem of our age, for so many of us are that way. Skiing provides a method, a means, of making the imbalance manifest, of bringing it out into a concrete situation where we can get our hands on it, grapple with it, and eventually prevail over it. My friend Lisa was unbalanced and she skied, I believe unconsciously, to experience her imbalance, to enlarge it, and to somehow go beyond it.

Lisa was a friend of mine with whom I had skied for several years, and then I moved to another area and lost contact with her. When I knew her she had been skiing for about six or seven years, but she wasn't much of a skier. Through long practice she had learned to ski a lot of difficult terrain, and she could even go down some fairly steep bump trails without falling. However, she had a very stiff, ungainly style. She held her skis very wide apart and appeared to be leaning way too far forward when she skied. She gave the appearance that she skied by force rather than skill.

Lisa was always trying to improve and occasionally took lessons at the ski school, but more often just asked for tips from her skiing friends, many of whom were expert skiers. Nothing she did seemed to improve her skiing much.

I remembered one conversation about skiing I had with Lisa and some of our friends. She had solicited comments on how she could improve, and I had offered the observation that she looked unusually stiff on her skis. "Have you ever tried stretching exercises?" I asked.

Lisa looked at me and said, "One thing I am not is stiff. Watch." She jumped up and stood with her feet close together and her knees locked, and then leaned forward, put the palms of her hands on the floor, and continued to lean until her elbows were only a couple of inches off the floor. Then she stood up.

"Well," I said, "so much for that idea. Anybody else want to try?"

After I lost contact with Lisa and began to develop my awareness techniques for teaching skiing, I found that I would think about her from time to time. Her body certainly wasn't stiff—if anything she was more flexible than 99% of the people on the slope—but she looked like one of the stiffest people I had ever seen on skis. It seemed to be a mystery. How could she be stiff and loose at the same time?

Then one day riding the lift with a friend of mine, I found out that Lisa was coming to our area for a visit.

"Is she going to ski while she's here?" I asked my friend. "Yeah," he said, "I think she is going to ski next Monday and Tuesday. A bunch of us are going to have dinner Sunday night after she gets in. Wanna come?"

"I'll be there," I said.

During the dinner I caught up with what had been going on with Lisa. She had kept skiing for the five years since I had last seen her. Recently she had been taking a special women's ski class. She was pretty enthusiastic about it. She began to describe some of the things she was doing in the class.

"Are you improving?" I asked Lisa.

"Yeah. Well, anyway, I think I am. At least the class is a lot of fun. I'm really enjoying myself on the mountain. The only thing I don't like is sometimes they tell us to do five or six different things on skis at once. I get mixed up and can't concentrate.

"But I hear that you're doing something new with ski instruction," she said. "Tell me about that."

I began to explain to Lisa some of my ideas about teaching skiing indirectly, instead of just demonstrating and asking the students to copy my movements, or giving them directions about the "right way" to ski. Lisa listened attentively.

After a while she interrupted me and said, "That sounds pretty neat. How about working with me while I'm here?"

"Sure," I said. "How about tomorrow morning?"

The next morning at ten o'clock we were on the hill. I picked a well-plowed intermediate-level trail to work on. I figured that Lisa would be insulted if I took her onto a beginner's trail. After all, she had been skiing for more than ten years.

"Make a few turns and let me see where you are," I told Lisa. She started to ski down the hill and I watched intently. As near as I could tell, she was skiing exactly the way she had been skiing five years before. She hadn't changed a bit. However, I didn't tell her that. It seemed like an inauspicious way to start a lesson.

I tried to analyze Lisa's skiing style as I watched. She was doing something peculiar that I couldn't quite put my finger on. I decided to work with the movement of turning about a vertical axis and just see where the lesson would lead.

I had Lisa stand still at the side of the trail and turn her whole body left and right. I had her turn all of the parts together, and then turn her head and eyes, and then her hips and shoulders, in opposite directions, and so on. As long as she was standing still or moving slowly across the trail, everything seemed to work perfectly. From time to time I would ask her to make a few turns, to see how the awareness movements were affecting her skiing. As soon as she started to ski, however, she would pitch forward, separate her skis, and stiffen up.

What was going on with Lisa? I couldn't quite figure it. But as I stood there watching her, I suddenly had an idea. I started to ski and as I did, I leaned far forward, just like Lisa. I felt my skis separate and my body get stiff. It was almost impossible to ski well with my weight that far forward. All my muscles became stiff trying to hold me up in that unbalanced posture.

Now I was pretty sure that I understood Lisa's problem. She was out of balance, leaning much too far forward, but she didn't *feel* that she was out of balance. And, what was equally important, she didn't feel that being out of balance affected her skiing in a particular way. The next step was to get Lisa to feel exactly what she was doing to unbalance herself so that she could correct herself. I thought the best way to do this would be to exaggerate Lisa's problem so she couldn't possibly ignore it.

"Hold up a second, I want to try something," I told her. "Go back to that full turning movement." Lisa began to turn her whole body left and right. "Keep turning and lean forward as far as you can, and feel what happens."

Lisa began to lean forward, and the farther she leaned, the less she was able to turn. "Can you feel that as you lean forward like that, the turning angle becomes constricted?" I asked Lisa.

"Yeah," she replied. "I can't turn nearly as far to the side when I lean forward like that."

"OK. Try it while you're leaning backward."

Lisa began to turn her body left and right, and as she did, she slowly leaned backward. As she leaned, I could see that she was able to turn her body less and less to each side. When she was leaning back as far as she could go, she could hardly turn at all. I pointed all this out to Lisa.

"I feel what you're talking about," she told me, "but what does it mean?"

"Well, think about it for a minute," I said. "When you lean forward, you can't turn your body very far left and right. When you lean backward, the same thing happens. So there must be a point somewhere in the middle, a kind of balance point, where the turning movement is easiest. Try leaning forward and back while you're turning and see if you can find the balance point."

Lisa began to turn left and right. As she turned, she would lean a little bit forward and then a little bit back, feeling how the position of her body affected the turning angle. Gradually, she leaned less and less, and finally she came to a stop at what appeared to me to be an excellent skiing posture.

"That's it," she said. "When I'm standing like this, I can turn easily. Any other position restricts the turning angle."

"How does that position feel to you?" I asked her.

"Well, it feels OK I guess, but this isn't the way that I usually stand when I ski. I think I stand leaning a little further forward."

"Now," I said to myself, "we're getting somewhere." I knew that Lisa leaned *much* too far forward when she skied. The point of all my maneuverings with her was to get her to feel that. Even though it seems incredible that someone could lean that far forward and not feel it, I felt certain that was the root of Lisa's problem. I knew that if I could get her to feel exactly how far forward she was leaning, exactly how far off balance she was, and exactly how much this imbalance affected her skiing, she would correct the problem herself.

"Good," I said. "Now, try that same thing, twisting your body left and right, while leaning forward and back, but this time ski very slowly across the trail."

Lisa began to ski slowly across the trail, leaning slowly forward and back while twisting left and right. I had her go back and forth for about a half hour like that. I wanted her to get the feeling of the balance point locked in tight.

Finally, I decided it was time. "Blow that off and just make a few turns," I told her. "Let's see what happens."

Lisa began to ski. As soon as she gathered a little speed and went into a turn, she pitched forward and separated her skis. She immediately stopped and looked at me. "Hey," she said, "do I lean too far forward when I ski?"

"Oh, maybe," I said nonchalantly. "What did you feel?"

"As soon as I started to turn, I felt myself pitch forward, into that position where it's hard to keep twisting my body. Do I do that all the time?" she asked, half to herself and half to me.

Lisa started to ski again, slowly, and I saw her pitch forward and stop several times, and then start out again. I just watched as she experimented. After about four tries, she managed to not pitch forward, and as she went into her turn, her skis stayed together and consequently she was able to turn much more quickly. Her skis whipped around in a quick parallel turn, and she stopped and looked at me. "What happened?" she asked.

"You just made a real parallel turn," I said. "How did it feel?"

"Like I was leaning way too far backward," she replied. "It was funny. It felt good and bad at the same time."

"Try a few more of those," I said. "Let's see what happens." Lisa began to ski, and as she turned she pitched forward and separated her skis again. She immediately stopped and said under her breath, "No, that's not it." She tried again, and this time she didn't pitch forward, and again she made an excellent parallel turn.

Then she did about five quick parallel turns in a row. Her feet stayed together, and her skis turned quickly and easily. She appeared to be relaxed and balanced as she turned. "Wow," she said. "I'm starting to feel it. I've been leaning way too far forward all these years. That's what's been messing up my skiing. But why was it I never felt it before?" she asked, looking at me.

"Well," I replied, "I don't really know. What I do know is that just about everybody who gets stuck and is unable to improve has some kind of 'blind spot' in their awareness—some part of their body or some movement that they are unable to feel. That blind spot blocks their learning. My job, when I'm teaching, is not just to tell my students what they're doing wrong, but rather to help them feel in themselves just what the problem is. Once they can feel it, the correction happens easily. With you, the problem was that you didn't feel you were leaning way too far forward, and that the leaning restricted your ability to twist your body and so hampered your turn. Sometimes it's hard to believe that a skier can be leaning twenty or thirty degrees forward of vertical or bending their spine into some strange angle and not feel it, but I have found over and over again that's the case. The important thing for me is that when I make someone aware of their problem, when I help them to feel it clearly in their own body, they correct themselves, spontaneously."

Summary

Here is a summary of the movements I did with Lisa to help her discover the balance point for turning.

1. Find a flat spot and set your poles down on the snow. Stand with your skis in a comfortable position, and your knees and hips bent a little. (Fig 9–1)

Fig 9–1

2. Begin to turn your whole body left and right. Let all the parts turn easily, and turn your head and eyes so that you look to one side and then the other as you turn. Spend a few minutes turning like this, and scan your body with your attention as you turn. Notice how far you turn to the side. (Fig 9–2A/B)

Fig 9–2A

Fig 9–2B

3. Now lean forward as far as you can, and continue to turn left and right. Notice how leaning forward like this inhibits your

ability to turn your body. Come back to your habitual stance and turn left and right a few more times, and then lean forward again, and so on, until you can feel exactly how leaning forward affects your ability to turn. (Fig 9–3A/B)

Fig 9–3A

Fig 9–3B

4. Now lean backward as far as you can, and continue to turn your body left and right. Notice how leaning backward also inhibits your ability to turn. Come back to your habitual stance, turn left and right a few times, then lean backward again, and so on. Continue until you can feel exactly how

Fig 9–4A

Fig 9–4B

leaning backward inhibits your ability to turn your body left and right. (Fig 9–4A/B)

5. Continue to turn your body to each side. As you turn, lean slowly forward and back. Each time, lean a little less forward and back until you can find the point in the middle, the balance point, where you can turn the maximum amount to the left and right. Stop turning and assess this stance. How does it compare to your usual skiing stance? Where does your weight fall on the bottoms of your feet? How much are your knees and hips bent?

6. Pick up your poles and try the above movements while skiing slowly across the hill. By doing this you can get the feeling of finding the balance point while you are moving. When the movement is clear, speed up a little and make some turns. Do you move away from the balance point when you start to turn? Can you keep your body at the balance point while turning? How does this improve your skiing?

10

Joy: The Unbendable Knee

The image many people have of a ski instructor is a blond, Nordic type whose favorite expression is "Bend zee kneez, pleeze!" And in fact, one of the biggest problems, almost a universal problem, affecting beginner and intermediate-level skiers is an inability to bend and straighten their knees easily while skiing.

Once the skier leaves the relative comfort and safety of the groomed trails and ventures onto a slope with some rough terrain or even worse, for those with stiff knees, bumps, the ability to bend the knees to absorb terrain changes becomes critical.

This particular problem had been annoying Joy for several years, and she had finally decided that bending the knees was "it" for her. "If I can just learn to bend my knees while I'm skiing, I'll be able to start improving again," she said to me.

We were sitting in the cafeteria drinking a cup of coffee and waiting for the lifts to open. There was about three or four inches of fresh powder on the slopes, and it looked like it was going to be a beautiful day. "Sometime today," Joy had told me, "I want you to fix my knees."

"While we're waiting," I said to Joy, "I want to try something. Stand up here by me and just bend and straighten your knees. I want to see how they move."

Joy stood up and began to bend and straighten her knees. "I don't have any problem with them when I'm not on skis," she said. I watched as she lowered herself almost down to the floor, bending her knees the maximum amount, and then stood up. She repeated the movement several times. "See?" she said,

"Nothing to it!"

"So why can't you bend them while you're skiing?" I asked.

"That's what I want *you* to tell *me*," she replied.

I looked at my watch. It was almost 9 A.M. "Well," I said, "Let's go get it." We got our gear and headed for the lift.

"What are you going to do?" asked Joy, as we rode up the lift.

"I'm not going to do anything," I replied. *"You* are. I'm just going to talk."

"What I mean is, what are we going to do about my knees?" she said.

"I've already got a pretty good idea what's wrong with your knees," I told Joy. "It's the same problem that just about every skier has. The details are different, but the root of the problem is the same just about every time."

"And just what is the 'root' of the problem, anyway?"

"Well, when you bend your knees, or when you *try* to bend them, I'll bet that you have your attention narrowed down almost to a point, so that you are thinking only about your knees, and not about what the rest of your body has to do to help the knees bend," I said. "When you bend your knees, you also have to do something with your ankles, hips, and spine. If you hold those parts tight, it's practically impossible to bend your knees. If you use a lot of effort and manage to force your knees to bend, you'll probably go off balance and fall."

"You've got my number," said Joy. "That's exactly what happens when I really try to bend my knees."

We were almost at the top. I asked Joy to get off and ski a couple of hundred yards down a groomed intermediate-level slope so that I could watch her style. Joy took off down the hill and I followed a little way behind her. She had a style like a lot of intermediate-level skiers that I see. She looked OK going down a groomed slope, where it doesn't matter a whole lot if your knees are stiff. But I could see a certain inflexibility in her movements that I knew would destroy her skiing if she were to have to ski over a few bumps, and try to bend and straighten her knees.

Joy stopped at the side of the trail, and I stopped beside her. "Are you ready for me to 'fix' your knees?" I asked.

"You bet," she replied.

Joy was standing just beside me in a relaxed stance, with her knees bent a little. "Unbuckle your boots," I told her.

Joy leaned over and unbuckled her boots. "Now," I said, "set your poles in the snow for balance, and then straighten your ankles so that you stand up on tiptoe, and then just relax so that you come back to the way you're standing now."

Joy began to do as I had said. I watched and noticed that as Joy stood up on tiptoe, she straightened her knees, actually locking them, and then she relaxed her knees as she bent her ankles.

"Why are you straightening your knees?" I asked Joy. "I didn't say anything about that."

She looked down at her knees. "I didn't realize I was straightening them," she said.

"Oh, really." I said. "I wonder if there are any other things you do that you don't notice." Joy had stopped moving. "Do that some more and just feel what your knees do."

Joy resumed the movement of standing up on tiptoe and then coming back to a normal stance. "This is really strange," she said. "I can feel my knees straightening and bending, but it's like I'm not doing it. What causes that, anyway?"

"I don't want to tell you right now," I said, "but remind me later and I'll explain it.

"Now, straighten your ankles like you just did, and hold them there. You should be able to feel that the balls of your feet are pressing down into your boots, and that your heels are lifted up off the boot." Joy pressed the balls of her feet down into her boots as if to stand on tiptoe, and she again straightened her knees. I pointed out that her knees were straight and stiff, just like when she was skiing.

"Hey, that's right!" she said. "Is that why I stiffen my knees when I ski?"

"Probably," I replied. "We'll find out for sure in the next few minutes.

"What I want you to do now is to hold your ankles stiff like that, with the ball of the foot pressed down, and then to bend and straighten your knees."

Joy began to get a pained expression on her face. "They won't bend!" she said.

"Just go real slowly, and loosen up your chest a little." I had noticed that she had stopped breathing.

Joy began to breathe, and simultaneously her knees started to bend a little. After a few minutes she was able to bend her knees easily while keeping her ankles straight and immobile.

"Good," I said. "Take a break and tell me how your legs feel."

She bounced up and down a few times. "They have a funny springy feeling," she told me. "It feels real nice."

"Now, let's try the opposite movement. Bend your ankles, so that the front of your foot is lifted up and your heel is pressed down."

Joy flexed her ankles, and simultaneously she bent her knees.

"Do you feel that when you straighten your ankles you straighten your knees, and that when you bend your ankles you bend your knees?" I asked her.

"Yeah," she said. "They seem to follow each other. Hey! I'll bet that if I tried to bend my ankles whenever I wanted to bend my knees, it would make my skiing go easier."

"You're getting ahead of me," I said. "That's about two more steps down the line.

"What I want you to try now is to hold your ankles bent like that, and then straighten and bend your knees."

Joy began to try the movement, and this time she was able to do it right away. I let her work with the movement for a few minutes, until it became familiar and easy to do.

"Now here's the clincher," I said. "The habitual way to move the ankles and knees is to move them together. When you straighten your ankles you straighten your knees, and when you bend your ankles you bend your knees. What I want you to do is to reverse that. Straighten your ankles, as if you were going to stand on tiptoe, and at the same time bend your knees. Then, bend your ankles and at the same time straighten your knees."

Joy began to try the movement I had just described. She had a strained look on her face. After a minute she stopped moving and burst out laughing. "Why is this so hard?" she said. "It sounds easy enough." She looked at me. "If I get this can you teach me to walk and chew gum at the same time?"

I laughed along with Joy. "We'll do that tomorrow," I promised her.

"Just try it slowly," I told her, "and don't hold your breath. It'll come in a minute."

After a few minutes of slow practice, Joy was able to do the movement.

"Now you've got it," I said. "The next thing is to learn to do that while you're skiing. So I want to go back over all those movements you just did while you're skiing very slowly across the slope. Go ahead and buckle up your boots, but not too tight. Give yourself a little slack so you can feel your ankles bend and straighten."

We spent about a half-hour repeating the movements of the knee and ankle while skiing very slowly across the slope. As I watched I could see Joy beginning to loosen up, and her whole body began to look light and springy. Finally we were back at the bottom.

"Come on and let's go back up," I said. "I think you're just about ready."

As we got on the lift Joy said, "I feel really light and springy, like I lost ten pounds. What causes that?"

"Your legs are starting to work like they should," I told her. "You always use them in only one way, and they get stuck.

"How do you mean 'only one way'?" she asked.

"Back in the real world, when you're not skiing, almost every move you make with the legs involves straightening and bending the knees and ankles together," I explained. "Walking, running, jumping, in all those activities the knees and ankles straighten and bend together. When you're skiing, however, you have to be able to straighten your ankles and bend your knees at the same time. But with most people their habit of moving the knees and ankles together is so locked in by years of doing it that way that some kind of special practice is required to get the legs to move easily when they're skiing.

"Try it here on the lift—you'll see it's the same, even when you're not standing up."

Joy straightened her ankles, pointing her toes, and her knees straightened out a little. "It sure is," she said.

"That's the explanation of why your knees straighten 'automatically'," I said to Joy. "It's just a habit. As long as you're not aware of it, you can't control it. We've been working the last hour to bring the habit into your awareness."

"But why would I point my toes in the first place?" she asked. "It seems like a funny thing to do."

"It's a leftover from the first days of learning to ski. Practically all beginners do that, point their toes, when they are first starting to ski, and most of them never completely get out of the habit." We were almost at the top.

"When we get off I'll show you what I mean," I told Joy.

At the top we got off the lift and skied over to the same intermediate trail. "Point your toes as hard as you can and try to ski," I told Joy.

She started to move, and as soon as she had gathered a little speed, she pitched her head forward and her butt back, straightened her knees, and began to do an awkward beginner's snowplow turn. She made about three turns and stopped. "Ugg!" she said. "That feels awful!"

"You've still got some of that stuck in your knees and ankles, and that's what's messing up your skiing," I said.

There was a little bump field over at the side of the trail. "Ski through those bumps and tell me how your knees feel now," I told Joy.

She looked at me. "No way," she said. "I am *not* a bump skier, and I never will be."

"I don't mean actually ski 'em, just go back and forth across the bumps on a slow traverse. That way you can feel the change in your knees."

She looked at me doubtfully. "OK, I'll try it if you say so."

Joy skied slowly over to the bumps. She came to almost a

complete stop and then entered the bump field at about two miles an hour. She slowly crossed the bumps and then turned around and came back. I expected her to let it go at that, but to my surprise she turned around and went across and back a second time, this time moving faster. She stopped and turned around, peering intently at the bumps. I skied down to stand beside her. "What's going on?" I asked.

"You know," she replied, "I almost always fall if I even *see* a bump, let alone hit one, but that was easy. I just glided over them like it was nothing. I've always been afraid to even try skiing bumps, but right now I feel I could learn, if I put some time into it. What's happened?"

"All we did was break up that habitual pattern of movement between your ankles and knees," I told her. "If you hit a bump with stiff knees, you're history, and your knees were always stiff. Now that they're free to bend, you just bend them when you need to, and it's easy."

"Well, it almost seems too easy," she said. "I've been trying to do that for years, and now, bang, nothing to it. I want to understand how I can change so quickly and easily."

"All we did was expand your awareness of that movement to include more of your body, in this case your ankles and feet. The body has to move as a whole, otherwise the parts fight each other and you get stiff."

"But you said the whole body has to be involved to make a movement easy. What about this part," she asked, indicating her torso with one hand. "We didn't do anything there."

"That's another lesson or two," I replied. "We can work there and improve the movement of the legs even more."

"I want to try that," Joy told me, "but not today. I think I've had enough."

"All right, I'll see you later," I said.

I skied a little way down the trail and then stopped and looked back at Joy. She was halfway across the bump field, and gaining speed.

Summary

Here is a summary of the movements I did with Joy to help her learn to use her knees easily while skiing. Try these movements first at home, wearing shorts, so you can see what you are doing. Put your hands on the back of a chair for balance. When the movements are clear, try them on skis. Try them first standing still, with your boots unbuckled, so you can make a big, easy-to-feel movement with your feet. Set your poles in the snow for balance as you do this. Finally, buckle your boots and try the movements while skiing slowly back and forth across an easy trail.

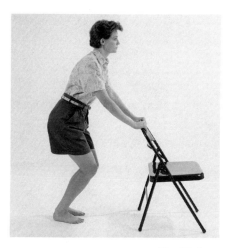

Fig 10–1

1. Stand up in your usual skiing posture, with your knees and hips bent comfortably. (Fig 10–1)

2. Straighten your ankles, lifting your heels off the floor, and then relax and let your heels come back down to the floor. Repeat this movement several times, and notice that as you straighten your ankles, your knees tend to straighten or even lock. Scan your body with your attention as you move, and be sure to let yourself breathe easily. (Fig 10–2)

Fig 10–2

3. Straighten your ankles, lifting your heels off the floor, and stop. Holding your ankles immobile, bend your knees as far as you can easily, and then straighten them. Repeat this movement about twenty times, and then relax and stand easily and rest. (Fig 10–3A/B)

Fig 10–3A

Fig 10–3B

4. Stand in your skiing posture again. Now, bend your ankles to lift the front of the feet off the floor, and then relax and let the front of your feet come back down onto the floor. Repeat this movement several times, and notice how you bend your knees as you bend your ankles. As usual, scan your body with your attention as you move. (Fig 10–4)

Fig 10–4

5. Bend your ankles, lifting the front of your feet up off the floor, and stop. Holding your ankles immobile, straighten and bend your knees about twenty times. Then relax and stand easily and rest briefly. (Fig 10–5A/B)

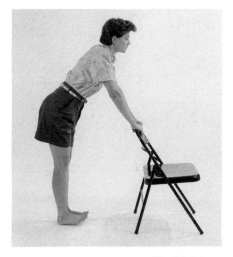

Fig 10–5A

Fig 10–5B

6. Again stand in your usual skiing posture. Straighten your ankles to lift your heels and stand on tiptoe, and then bend your ankles to lift the front of your feet off the floor. Continue to bend and straighten your ankles, and notice how the knees follow the ankles: when you straighten the ankles the knees straighten, and when you bend the ankles, the knees bend. Continue and exagger-

Fig 10–6A

ate the movement of the knees so that they bend and straighten a little more than they usually do. (Fig 10–6A/B)

7. Rest briefly, and then go back to your skiing posture. Once again bend and straighten your ankles, as you just did, but this time reverse the movement of the knees: as you straighten the ankles to stand on tiptoe, bend your knees; then, as you bend the ankles to lift the front of the feet off the floor, straighten your knees. Even though this

Fig 10–6B

is a simple movement, you may find that several minutes of slow, careful practice are required before you are able to do it easily. Stand up and take a rest. Jump up off the floor a few inches. How do your legs feel as you jump? (Fig 10–7A/B)

Fig 10–7A

Fig 10–7B

8. The next time you are on skis, try these movements standing still, with your boots unbuckled, and holding your poles for balance. Then buckle your boots and try the movements while skiing slowly across the trail. Remember to scan your body with your attention as you move, and to let yourself breathe easily. When the movement is clear in your awareness, try skiing slowly across an easy bump field. How do your legs feel as you go over the bumps? Get on an easy slope without any bumps and make a few turns. Feel how your ankles and knees bend and straighten together as you turn. How does your improved awareness of how your ankles and knees work together affect your skiing?

$$11$$

Ralph: The Straight Back

The human body is a wonderful piece of equipment, but very few people ever learn to use it well. One of the biggest obstacles to overcome is the idea that we really know what we are doing. Most of us assume that if we feel we are bending our knees or our hip joints, for example, we are in fact doing just that, and nothing else.

In our everyday life, walking back and forth from the car or occasionally jogging a few miles, we can live with this illusion that we know what we are doing with our bodies. However, if we try to reach for a higher level of ability, we become stuck. All our efforts to improve are thwarted.

This is the situation with most intermediate-level skiers. The more they try to improve, the more they become entrenched in their faulty mode of skiing. But most of these skiers would give little credence to the idea that their main problem is not knowing what they are doing with their bodies. That is, what they *feel* they are doing and what they are *actually* doing are two different things.

This turned out to be exactly the problem with one of my students, whose name was Ralph.

Watching him ski, the most obvious thing I noticed about his style was that he rounded his back, by contracting the muscles in the front of his body. I knew this would cause several problems.

To begin with, when the back is rounded in this way, with the middle of the spine curved too far backward, the lungs don't have room to expand and breathing is inhibited. Also, when the spine is curved like this, in order to see where you are going, you must lift your head by bending your neck backward. This puts a real strain on the neck muscles, and causes pain there.

The final problem is more subtle. The human spine is able to do its job of bearing weight easily only if it is held in a particular configuration. This is usually referred to as a "straight back," even though in this position the spine is not actually straight like a ruler. There are two gentle curves inward and one outward. The inward curves are at the neck and lumbar (small of the back) areas. In between these two inward curves there is an outward curve in the area of the shoulder blades. If you lie flat on your back on the floor you should be able to feel these curves. Your neck and lumbar areas will arch off the floor, and the area between the shoulder blades will press strongly into the floor.

Chiropractors managed to figure this out years ago, and they began to publish posters demonstrating the "Proper Way to Lift a Heavy Object." I have seen a number of these signs, usually posted in warehouses, or anywhere heavy lifting is done. They all have a drawing of a human figure lifting a large box by bending at the hips and knees, and keeping a "straight back."

If you pretend you are going to lift a heavy object according to the directions of the chiropractors, and squat about halfway down, and then lean a little forward, you will be in an almost perfect skiing posture.

The idea is that the spine will be able to take the added weight easily if all the force is directed along the axis of the spine, from the head straight down to the pelvis, and none of the force is directed sideways. (An engineer would say that the spine is loaded in compression, and that there are no shearing forces.)

In the middle of a parallel turn, the effective weight of the body is quite a bit more than the real weight, because of the centrifugal force generated by the turn. Thus, the situation in the spine is almost the same as if you were lifting a heavy weight. And if you watch a good skier, you will see that he doesn't bend his spine unnecessarily.

However, all this information is meaningless if you are unable to feel whether or not your spine is bent or straight. And to do that, curiously enough, you have to know where your hip joints are.

I yelled down the hill at Ralph to "Hold it!" and I skied over to him and stopped. He was rubbing his neck and grimacing painfully. "Bingo," I said to myself.

"Is your neck bothering you?" I asked Ralph.

"Yeah," he replied. "It seems like it hurts most of the time when I'm skiing."

"Most of the complaints I hear are about legs," I said. "I wonder why your neck hurts."

"I don't know," he said wearily, "But it's a real bother."

"Get into your skiing stance," I told Ralph, "and I'll show you why it hurts."

Ralph bent his knees to crouch down as if to ski, but instead of bending his hip joints, he rounded his back by bending his spine in the lumbar region. With his spine curved in this way, he had to contract the muscles in the back of his neck to look up and see the slope. I stepped over to Ralph and squeezed the muscles at the back of his neck gently. They felt hard and stringy. Ralph winced as I squeezed. I told him to stand up.

"When you go into your skiing stance," I asked him, "you bend your knees, of course, but where else do you bend?"

Ralph replied, "At the hips, of course."

"Show me with your hands where you bend at the hips," I said.

With one hand, Ralph indicated a point on his right side near his ribs, about six inches above his hip joint. "Are you sure that's where your hip joint is?" I asked him.

"Well, yeah, it's about there," he said.

"Lift your right leg and set it down a few times, and notice where you bend to lift the leg. In fact, look at your leg to see where it bends, or where the hip joint is, which is the same thing."

Looking, Ralph could see that his hip joint was actually about six inches lower than he had indicated with his hand.

"That's the big problem with your skiing," I said to Ralph. "You feel as if your hip joint is about six inches higher than it actually is, and so you bend your body in the wrong place, and that throws everything off."

Ralph looked at me and stepped back a foot. "Hold it, hold it," he said, waving his hands in front of his face as if to clear away some obstruction. "I'm getting lost. I came out here to learn to ski better, and you starting talking about why my neck hurts, and now you say I don't know where my hip joints are. What's all this got to do with my skiing better?"

"All those things—your skiing problems, your aching neck, and your hip joints—are connected in a very precise way. They are all elements of your problem. They are not separate from each other, or from you as a person, for that matter. What I want to do now is to help you find out exactly how they are connected, and how they affect your skiing. When you can feel exactly how all the parts of that pattern fit together, you will be able to change it for the better. As long as you are thinking in a fragmented way about this piece and that piece, and some other piece, and not thinking about the connections that make up the whole, you are going to be stuck."

"OK," Ralph said, "Let's give it a try."

We went over to the side of the trail. I took his poles and pushed the tips down into the snow. Each pole was just to the outside of his skis, and about a foot and a half in front of the toes of his boots. Ralph watched me with a look of incredulity on his face.

"I'll say one thing," he remarked, "this is sure the weirdest ski lesson I've ever had."

"Grab your pole grips," I said, "and lean forward until your shoulders are resting on the very top of the grips, and bend your knees as much as you need to be comfortable."

Ralph rolled his eyes upward, as if to say "What next?" and then did as I asked.

I looked at Ralph. He was in a kind of modified skiing posture. His knees were bent as if he were skiing, but his torso was almost horizontal, with the front of his shoulders resting on his poles. He had curved his spine just like he did when he skied.

"How does your neck feel?" I asked him.

"It's already starting to hurt," he said. "Just like when I ski."

"Take a deep breath, and tell me how that feels."

Ralph inhaled, making a kind of wheezing sound. "It's hard to breathe like this," he said.

"OK," I said, "now we are going to get down to the nitty gritty." I got close to Ralph and pushed down gently on the middle of his spine. "Let your belly drop and think about arching your back a little," I said. "Just follow the pressure of my hand on your back."

Ralph struggled for a few seconds, and I let him be. I knew that this movement, although an easy one, was very unfamiliar to him. I gave him all the time he needed. Suddenly he dropped the middle of his torso down, and let out a big sigh.

He had transferred the bending in the middle of his body from the lumbar region of his spine to his hip joints, where it should be.

Now that his spine was relatively straight, the strain was off his neck. "How does your neck feel now?" I asked Ralph.

Gingerly, he moved his head around a little. "The strain is off," he said. "It feels relaxed now."

"Check your breathing," I said.

Again Ralph took a deep breath. This time I didn't hear the wheezing noise. "All of a sudden it's a lot easier to breathe," he said.

"OK, stand up and take a rest."

Ralph stood up. "You know," he remarked, "that position that you just had me in felt real strange. Like I was out of kilter, somehow. And why was I leaning on my poles? What was that for?"

"When you lean on the poles," I said, "your spine has some support at each end, instead of only one end, and the muscles along there are not working so hard, so they are able to go into a different configuration more easily. You wouldn't have been able to move your spine like that if I had just had you lean over without some support.

"And the position feels strange to you because you never allow yourself to get into that position. Using your spine in that way is foreign to you. It's like you have excluded some part of yourself. You don't really own your own back."

"So what do we do now? Do I just go ski and try to bend in that new place? Is that all there is to it?"

"That's just the beginning," I told Ralph. "If I just let you go straight back to skiing, your old habits would force you back into your old way of skiing. We have to sneak up on this a little at a time."

"I've got a strong feeling that you're on the right track," said Ralph. "There was something about my spine that felt *right* just a minute ago, but it would be tough to say exactly what it is."

"We all have an internal feeling of what's right and wrong, Ralph, but we learn to cover it up and deny it. But it's still there, and if you go about it in the right way, you can recover it.

"So bend over, and rest your shoulders on the pole grips again."

Ralph grasped the pole grips and leaned forward as I had said.

"Look down, drop your head, and round your back," I told Ralph. I was asking him to exaggerate his usual skiing posture, so that he could feel it more easily.

"I feel like an angry cat when I stand like this," he said.

"Yeah," I replied, "Sometimes I call this the 'cat back' exercise. Now go the other way, look up, drop your belly down, and arch your back." As Ralph moved, I used my fingers along his spine, touching places that appeared to be stiff to help him get some movement there.

"Now just keep doing that, look up and arch your back, and then look down and round your back, and feel how your whole spine bends one way and then the other. And of course your head and pelvis, which are attached to the spine, move also. Pay particularly attention to your pelvis, so that you can feel how you bend at the hip joints." I watched as Ralph flexed and extended his spine, the movement becoming smoother and easier with each repetition.

"Stop with your back rounded," I said. "Now just move your head and eyes only, and look up and down about a dozen times. Slowly."

"Now do a few more movements of rounding your back and arching it, while looking down and up . . . and then stop with your back arched, looking up. Good. Now hold your back arched and again move your head and eyes and look down and up about a dozen times." I watched as Ralph moved.

"OK," I said, "go back to the movement of arching your back and then rounding it, and just notice exactly how your back feels now." I could see the movement of Ralph's spine was enlarged now, indicating that some of the unnecessary tension had been removed. Also, he was tilting his pelvis easily on his hip joints.

"Do a few more of those movements, flexing and extending your whole spine, and then stop with your back arched like a cat, and with your head and eyes looking down.

"Now, keep everything still except your eyes, and move your eyes and look up and down about fifteen or twenty times. And be sure to breathe."

I watched as Ralph did as I asked. "Now put your back into the other position, arched, with your belly dropped down, and looking up. Then hold your whole body still and move your eyes and look up and down about twenty times again."

Finally I asked Ralph to arch and round his back a few more times. The movement appeared to be easy, smooth, and fluid.

Ralph stood up and stretched, letting out a big sigh. "Man," he remarked, "my back feels great! I think I'm an inch taller!"

"Grab your poles and let's keep going," I instructed him.

I had Ralph stand facing across the trail. "Now just bend your knees and hips as if to squat down, and then stand up. And as you squat, think about arching your back a little."

Ralph began to squat down and then stand up. I watched and could see that now he was bending at the hips and not in the lumbar region.

"Keep doing that and just ski very slowly across the trail," I told him.

I had Ralph ski back and forth across the trail for almost a half-hour, all the while bending and then straightening his hips and knees. I asked him to arch his back and look up as he bent his knees and hips, and then to reverse the movement of the spine and round his back and look down as he bent his knees and hips. As the movements became easy and familiar, I had him lean forward a little and then back, and then to do it with most of his weight on one ski, and then the other. Finally I had him speed up a little. He didn't have any trouble carrying out any of my instructions.

We were on a flat, easy section of trail. "OK," I told Ralph, "Make some turns and let's see how you do."

Ralph took off and began a series of parallel turns. He looked great. I skied up beside him. "How is it?" I asked.

"I don't want to stop," he said, shaking his head from side to side, "I'm in heaven!"

I dropped back and watched Ralph cruise down the hill. Later that afternoon I saw him in the bar with some of his friends. He was sitting on a chair at a table, arching and rounding his back as he talked. I edged closer so I could hear what he was saying.

"That's right," he said to his friends, who appeared to be listening intently, "All you have to do is put your back into it, like this," he demonstrated, "and skiing's a piece of cake."

Summary

Here is a summary of the movements I did with Ralph to help him get his back organized properly for good skiing.

1. Find a flat spot where the snow is fairly soft so you can push your poles down into it a few inches. Place the tip of each pole in the snow about eighteen inches in front of the toe of the boot, and just to the outside of the ski. Grab the poles and then lean forward and place the front of each shoulder on top of the pole handle for support. Adjust your position until you

feel that the poles are supporting your upper body. (Fig 11–1)

2. Begin to flex and extend your back. Drop your head, look down, and round your back like an angry cat; then look up with your head and eyes, and drop your stomach down to arch your back. Continue to do this move, slowly and easily, and be sure to breathe. As you move, scan your body

Fig 11–1

with your attention. Pay particular attention to your spine. Notice if the whole spine moves easily or if some parts feel stiff, as if they are not participating in the movement. Can you feel your pelvis tilting up and down as you round and arch your back? Measure how far your spine bends by noticing how far you can look up and down. (Fig 11–2A/B)

Fig 11–2A

Fig 11–2B

3. Now, stop moving with your back arched. You are looking up, and your belly is dropped down. Keeping your entire body still, move your head and eyes and look up and down, slowly, about

twenty times. Then repeat the movement of rounding and arching the back a few more times. (Fig 11–3A/B)

Fig 11–3A   *Fig 11–3B*

4. Now, stop moving with your back rounded. You are looking down, and your belly is sucked in. Keeping your entire body still, move your head and eyes and look up and down, slowly, about twenty times. Then repeat the movement of rounding and arching the back a few more times. How does the movement feel now? Can you look further up and down? If so, that means some of the excess tension in your back has been removed. (Fig 11–4A/B)

Fig 11–4A   *Fig 11–4B*

5. Stand up and rest for a minute. Then bend over and rest your shoulders on the poles again. Round and arch your back a few more times. Stop with your back rounded, so that your belly is sucked in and your head is dropped down. Hold this position, and moving only your eyes, look up and down about twenty times. Then arch and round your back a few more times. (Fig 11–5A/B)

Fig 11–5A   Fig 11–5B

6. Stop moving with your back arched, so that your belly is dropped down and you are looking up. Hold your body still, and moving only your eyes, look up and down another twenty times. Finally, arch and round your back, moving your head, eyes, spine, and pelvis, a few more times. Notice how much further you can look up and down now. Even more of the excess tension has been removed from the back. You will now be able to use the increased range of motion in your back in your skiing. (Fig 11–6A/B)

7. Stand up and remove your poles from the snow. Bend and straighten your knees and hips a few times. How does this movement feel? Bend your knees and hips so that you are in your usual skiing posture. Gently, try the movement of rounding and arching the back in this position while looking up and down. You will find that you cannot make as big a movement

Fig 11–6A   Fig 11–6B

while standing up like this, because without the poles to support your weight, your muscles are working to keep you upright. Repeat the movement a few times, until it feels easy, and then begin to ski slowly across the trail. Make several traverses while arching and rounding your back. Try it with your weight on your toes, and with your weight on your heels. (Fig 11–7A/B)

Fig 11–7A   Fig 11–7B

8. Continue to ski slowly across the trail, while you bend and straighten your knees and hips. As you bend your knees and

hips, round your back and look down; as you straighten your knees and hips, arch your back and look up. (Fig 11–8A/B)

Fig 11–8A

Fig 11–8B

9. Continue to ski slowly across the trail while bending and straightening your knees and hips. As you bend your knees and hips, arch your back and look up; as you straighten your knees and hips, round your back and look down. (Fig 11–9A/B)

Fig 11–9A

Fig 11–9B

10. Finally, make a few turns on an easy slope. Experiment with the position of your back as you turn. How does the configuration of your back affect your skiing?

12

Bob: The Case of the Wandering Feet

Bob shared a problem with many other skiers: he couldn't keep his feet together while turning. "In the middle of a turn," he told me, "my feet separate no matter how hard I try to keep them together."

From my experience teaching, I knew there could be many reasons for a person to separate his feet while skiing. Beginners, of course, all do this, because they feel insecure when they first get on skis. It's a natural human reaction. When we began to learn to stand and walk as infants, our first stance is with feet wide apart. As we learn and grow, we become more comfortable in our new, upright position, and we spontaneously bring our feet together without having to be told to do it.

Skiers go through this same progression as they learn. The beginner holds his feet very wide apart and uses a wedge turn. The intermediate holds his feet fairly close together on the traverse and separates them a little as he does his stem turn. The advanced skier keeps his feet together almost all the time, only separating them, for example, to make a wedge turn in close conditions, like a lift line.

Thus, for the majority of skiers, an inability to keep the feet together during a turn isn't the primary problem. It's more like the symptom of the real problem, which can be viewed as an inability to feel comfortable, balanced, and secure on skis.

As a result, with most of the skiers I work with, I never have to do anything specifically to get them to bring their feet together. Keeping the feet together develops naturally as overall balance and skill on skis improve.

Watching Bob ski, however, I saw something different. His balance looked good, and he appeared to be relaxed on his skis. But still, he separated his skis when he made a turn.

"Come over here," I said to Bob. "I want to show you something." Bob skied over to the side of the trail and stopped beside me.

"Get into your skiing stance, knees bent, skis together, and uphill ski leading a little." Bob crouched down into his stance, right ski uphill. "Now," I told him, "slide your uphill ski about six inches out in front of your downhill ski. From that position, move your knees apart and together by tilting your skis to the outside edges and then to the inside edges a few times." I watched as Bob did as I asked.

"OK. Now move your uphill ski back about one inch and move your knees apart and together again."

I watched as Bob moved. I let him move his knees apart and together by tilting his skis onto their outside and then inside edges several times, and then I asked him to slide his uphill ski back another inch, and again move his knees apart and together, and so on. As he did this, his right knee moved progressively backward, coming closer and closer to his left knee. Soon the two knees were beginning to touch.

"What I want you to try to do," I told Bob, "is to find a position where your knees fit together just like your hands fit together when you interlace your fingers. Just keep sliding your right knee backward a little bit and then moving your knees apart and together until you get it."

Bob began to move very slowly, concentrating on the movement of his knees. After a few minutes he said, "I think I've got it. Does this look right?"

"Yeah," I said, "that looks right. What do you feel?"

Bob separated his knees and reached down with one hand to feel them. "There's a kind of a groove on the right front side of the left knee when it's bent, between the knee cap and the side of the knee. And on the right side, there's a kind of rope of muscle that sticks out when you bend the knee. The two fit right into each other, just like they were made to go there."

"Right," I said. "And they only fit perfectly when the knee that is out in front is about an inch higher than the other knee. And that only happens when you are skiing, as far as I know. It almost looks like the human body has evolved to ski."

"I wonder what Darwin would think of that idea?" Bob said.

"Probably not much," I admitted. "But let's keep working. Put your knees back together so that the muscle of the right leg fits into the groove on the left knee."

Bob put his knees together. "Notice that when you do that, your skis are in exactly the position that the ski instruction manuals describe. The uphill ski is just a little forward of the downhill ski, and the curved tip of the downhill ski blocks the uphill ski so that you don't cross your tips. Now, keep your knees together like that, and move both knees from side to side, so that you tilt your skis a little left and right on the snow."

Bob began to move his knees left and right. "As you do that," I continued, "let your attention move from your feet slowly up through your legs and on up through your torso, to your shoulders and head. Just make sure that you aren't holding any part stiff."

I gave Bob plenty of time to feel how his whole body was involved in the movement of the knees. As I watched, I could see the motion become smoother, easier, and more graceful.

"Good," I said. "Now turn around and try that same thing with the left ski uphill. That way, the back of the left knee will fit into the groove in the left front side of the right knee."

Bob spent a few more minutes working to fit his knees together, this time with his left ski uphill.

"OK," he said. "I've got it. What now?"

"Put your knees together," I told him, "and ski very slowly across the hill. As you move, keep your knees together and just move them left and right as far as they will go easily."

I watched as Bob began to ski slowly across the hill. I followed close behind him. After a few traverses I began to direct his attention to other parts of his body. "Can you feel what your hips are doing?" I asked. "How about your spine, and your ribs, and your neck? Is there any part of the movement where you hold your breath?" As Bob began to feel how his whole body was involved in the motion of moving the knees from side to side, the movement became easy and graceful, and nice to look at.

I asked Bob to stop on an easy section of trail. "Now I want you to try this," I told him. "Make a few turns. When you come into the turn, you'll have one knee locked into the groove of the other. As you turn, slide the knees around so that the other knee is in front. As you do that, concentrate on your thighs. Feel how they press together, and how the pressure moves around on the inside of each thigh as you change the knees over."

Bob began to ski easily down the hill, with his knees locked together. As he turned, he slid the knees one around the other, keeping them together. With his knees locked together like that, his feet also stayed together.

I followed behind Bob for about fifteen or twenty turns. Finally he stopped. I skied up beside him. "How was that?" I asked.

"That feels really good," he said. "My turns have never felt so easy. I felt like I was floating down the hill."

"Good," I said, looking at my watch. "We've got a few more minutes—is there anything else you want to work on?"

"But how about my . . . Hey! I had my feet together during those turns! I didn't even notice it! What happened?"

"Well," I said, "the muscles that pull the legs together run from the lower bones of the pelvis to the thigh, and they attach to the inside of the thigh in several places, ending up down at the knees. They're called the adductor muscles. So to put your feet together, you actually have to put your knees together. If you're thinking only about pulling your feet together, you will be misdirecting the muscular power of the legs. The whole point of the exercise I had you do was to get you to feel how the knees can come together. To change the way you move yourself, you have to change the way you feel yourself.

"In fact," I continued, "that's the 'hidden variable' in skiing. Some people ski well, and a lot more people get stuck at a low level of ability. If you watch a good skier, you can see *that* he skis well, but not *why*. The difference is in what part of the body each skier pays attention to, and you can't see that just by watching.

"So if you try to copy a good skier without knowing how he experiences his body, and how he directs himself to move, you probably won't succeed.

"In general, you need to use your whole body in a very specific way to ski well, and most skiers pay attention to just one or two parts as they ski. Thus, they are using only a small fraction of their potential. When I'm teaching, I try to find what parts are outside the student's awareness when he skis, and to devise a means to bring other parts into use. When I do that, the skiing improves spontaneously. That's really all there is to it."

Summary

Here's a summary of the movements I did with Bob to help him keep his skis together.

1. Stand still at the side of an easy trail, with the uphill direction to your right. Bring your skis together, with the tip of the right ski about six inches in front of the tip of the left ski. (Fig 12–1)

Fig 12–1

2. Tilt both skis to their outside edge, and then to their inside edge. Notice how your knees move sideways away from each other and then closer together. (Fig 12–2A/B)

Fig 12–2A   Fig 12–2B

3. Move your right ski about an inch backward, and then repeat the previous sideways movement of the knees a few times. (Fig 12–3A/B) Continue to move the right ski backward an inch at a time, until you find a position of the skis where the knees fit

Fig 12–3A   Fig 12–3B

together, almost like the hands fit together when you interlace your fingers, or like your arms fit together when you fold them across your chest.

4. When you find that position, hold your knees locked together, and move both knees left and right a few times. Notice how your skis tilt left and right as you do this. Continue to move, and scan your body with your attention. What can you feel in your hips, your spine, your ribs, and your neck? (Fig 12–4A/B)

Fig 12–4A   Fig 12–4B

5. Turn around and try these movements with the left ski uphill, and fit the left front side of the right knee into the right rear side of the left knee. When the knees fit together, move them left and right a few times and feel how the skis tilt left and right. As usual, scan your body with your attention as you move the knees.

6. Ski slowly back and forth across the slope with your knees locked together. As you ski, move your knees slowly from side to side and notice how your skis tilt left and right.

7. Make a few turns on an easy slope and hold your knees locked together in the way that you have learned. How does holding your knees together like this affect your skiing?

13

Kathy: Whither the Poles?

Riding up on the lift with Kathy, she told me about her "biggest problem" in skiing.

"It's my poles," she said, "I just don't know what to do with them. I've read in books what you're *supposed* to do, but when I try it, it feels awkward and throws me off balance."

Kathy's problem sounded interesting to me. I couldn't wait to watch her ski.

Finally the chair arrived at the top. I pointed out an easy trail and asked Kathy to make a few turns so I could see what her "pole problem" looked like.

Kathy put on her pole straps, took a deep breath, and started down the hill. As soon as she started to move, she extended both arms straight out to the side, with her poles hanging straight down. From the back, she looked almost exactly like a scarecrow. Somehow, she managed to force her skis to turn a little, but it was an awkward, slow turn. Watching her ski, I got the distinct impression that her arms were just getting in her way.

Kathy stopped and I skied up beside her. "See what I mean?" she said. "When I'm skiing, I almost wish I didn't have arms. They just get in the way."

"I see exactly what you mean," I told her. "Just hang on a minute while I think about what to do with you."

My guess about Kathy was that she didn't feel how the movements of her arms affected the rest of her body, and vice versa. I knew that the human arm is connected to the body by only one bone, the collar bone, or clavicle. This is the sole bony connection between the arm and the rest of the body.

However, the arm is connected by many muscles to the rest of the body. In particular, in the back, muscles come from the shoulder and attach to the skull, all along the spine and ribs, and to the pelvis.

For effective use of the arms and poles, then, a skier needs to be able to feel how the movement of the head, spine, ribs, and pelvis affects the movements of the arms and shoulders, and vice versa. Thinking in this way gave me an idea of how to begin to work with Kathy.

Kathy was standing with her skis perpendicular to the fall line, and with the uphill direction to her right. "Plant your poles in the snow about shoulder-width apart, and just a little in front of yourself," I told her. "You can keep your hands on the grips for balance. Now, bring your feet together, with your uphill ski leading, and bend your knees as if you were in a skiing posture.

"OK. From that position, move your knees to the right, in the uphill direction, as if you were going to set your edges, and then move them back to neutral."

I watched as Kathy moved her knees from side to side. It was an easy movement, and I could see that she wasn't having any trouble doing it. However, I could also see that her upper body wasn't involved in the motion at all. Her hips, spine, ribs, shoulders, and head appeared to be disconnected from the movement of her knees.

"Hold it a second," I said. Kathy stopped moving and stood up. "Tell me something—when you move your knees to the side, what do you do with your upper body?"

Kathy made a face, and tilted her head to one side. "Beats me," she replied.

"Try that same movement again, and pay attention to what you do with the rest of your body," I said.

Kathy bent her knees and began to move them from side to side. She had an intense look on her face, as if she were concentrating on some difficult problem.

Finally she stopped moving and stood up. "I'm not really sure what I do with my upper body," she told me. "I can feel that it moves a little, but I'm not sure just how. Does that have something to do with my arms?"

"It has *everything* to do with your arms," I said, "and now we're going to fix 'em up. But first, move your knees to the right, or set your uphill edges, which amounts to the same thing, and just measure how far your knees move to the side."

Kathy did as I asked and said that her knees moved "about three or four inches" to the side.

"Good," I said. "Now bend your knees again, as if you were skiing." Kathy crouched down into her skiing posture.

"OK, now bring your left hip and shoulder closer together, and then come back to neutral. Just do that movement a few times."

I watched as Kathy attempted to do the movement I had described. At first she appeared to be having a rough time. She swayed around and moved her body from side to side without actually bringing her left hip and shoulder closer together. This was about what I expected. I had asked her to do a movement that was unclear in her awareness, and she couldn't do it right away.

"In order to do that," I said to her, "you have to bend your spine to the side. So just think about the left side of your body getting shorter and the ribs compressing on that side, and think of the right side getting longer and the ribs fanning out."

As Kathy changed her thinking, she began to change her movement. Now she was starting to do the movement I had described. Also, I noticed, as she bent her spine to the side, she was starting to move her knees to the right. That is, she was starting to feel how her whole body was involved in the edging movement. However, she hadn't yet begun to move her shoulders, which was the particular thing I was looking for.

"Keep moving," I said, "and think about your neck. Your neck is part of your spine, and you can let it bend along with the rest of your spine as you move. As you bring your left hip and shoulder closer together, tilt your head so that your left ear comes closer to your left shoulder."

As Kathy added the movement of her head to the movement of the rest of her body, the whole movement became bigger, smoother, and easier. Now she was really bending to the side.

After she had made about twenty movements like this, I asked her to stop while she was bent all the way over to the left.

"Hold your body in that position," I told her, " and just tilt your head left and right about a dozen times. Bring your right ear closer to your right shoulder, and then tilt your head the other way, so that your left ear comes closer to your left shoulder."

As Kathy tilted her head left and right, her shoulders finally started to move, following her head. They had been almost stationary up to this point.

"Keep moving your head," I said, "and notice that you're beginning to move your shoulders. Tell me just what they're doing."

Kathy kept moving, and after a minute she said, "They're following the movement of my head. When my head tilts left, so do my shoulders, and vice versa."

"Good. Now we're getting somewhere. Keep moving, and just exaggerate the movement of your shoulders a little."

"Whew," said Kathy, after a minute, "my legs are getting tired."

"Stand up and take a rest," I told her. She stood up and rolled her shoulders around a little. A questioning look appeared on her face. "What did you do to my shoulders? They feel real peculiar."

"I think they're starting to wake up," I said. "Let's do one more thing. Bend your whole body to the side like you were just doing. Let your left hip and shoulder come closer together, and at the same time move your left ear toward your left shoulder, and let your shoulders follow your head.

"In other words, bend your whole body to the left. And as you do that, notice what your knees do."

Kathy began to bend, and as she did, her knees moved over to the right, setting her uphill edges.

"Just notice how your knees move over to the right," I told her, "and notice how far they move now."

"Wow," she said, "they move about three or four times as far as they did before. I'll bet that will really help my skiing."

"Keep doing that side bending movement," I told her, "and as you move, think that the main purpose of the movement is to move your knees to the side, and that the rest of the body just follows the knees. Do that for a minute or so.

"Now, continue to move, and think that the main idea is to bend the spine to the side. Do that for another minute.

"Now, finally, think that the main purpose of the movement is to move the left ear closer to the left shoulder. They're all really the same movement, bending the whole body to the side, but I want you to feel how all the parts of the body work together to make the motion smooth, easy, big, and powerful."

Kathy stood up. "There at the end, I had the strangest feeling. I can't quite put it into words. Something shifted, and I felt that my whole body was moving differently. All the parts kind of 'connected up' together. Whatever it is, it sure feels nice."

"Close your eyes," I told her, "and feel your whole body. Compare the left side with the right."

Kathy shut her eyes and stood still for a minute. A look of wonderment stole over her face. She opened her eyes. "My left side feels like it's about twice as big as my right side. I'm completely lopsided!"

"Yeah," I said, "I just want you to feel what a little awareness can do. My motto is, 'A little awareness goes a long way.'"

"Now," I continued, I don't want to leave you lopsided, so turn around and do that same sequence of movements on the other side, so that you move your knees to the left and shorten the right side of your body. If you can't remember everything you did, I'll be right here so you can ask."

I watched as Kathy turned around and repeated the movements, shortening the right side of her body. Everything went smoothly.

"OK," I said. "Now the next trick is to integrate that side-bending movement into your skiing. So, just ski very slowly across the slope and do that same movement, bending to the side, but don't bend so far, since you won't have your poles planted in the snow for balance."

I watched as Kathy began to ski slowly across the slope. The uphill direction was to her right, and so she was bending to shorten her left side. At the side of the trail she stopped, turned around, and began to ski slowly back toward me, this time bending to shorten her right side. I noticed that she wasn't holding her arms straight out to the side now. She had dropped them down and bent her elbows a little.

At first, she hardly bent her body at all, because the movement felt unfamiliar to her. But after a few traverses, she was bending easily quite a bit to each side. I skied close by her, directing her attention to first one part of her body, then another.

The more she bent, I noticed, the more her arms relaxed. Finally, after about a half-hour of traverses, she began to "walk" her poles, planting one and then the other, as she slowly skied across the trail.

"What are you doing with your poles?" I asked her.

She looked at her poles and then stopped. "Uh, I don't know," she replied.

"Ski like that a little more," I directed, "and just notice what you're doing with your poles."

Kathy resumed her slow traverse, watching her poles. She stopped again and looked at me. "My arms are doing something, but I don't feel like I'm doing it. It almost feels like someone else is moving my arms." She shuddered. "It feels weird. What's going on?"

"I think your arms are waking up. They're getting connected to the rest of your body. That's actually the trick. When your body is organized more or less correctly, you tend to do the 'right' moves naturally, almost without instruction. All the work we've done up to now has been to get you to feel how your back muscles have to be organized to bend to the side and set your edges. And since a lot of the back muscles attach to the shoulders or the shoulder blades, your arms are starting to work.

"And as a fringe benefit, you can now do the movement of edging about three or four times as well as you could an hour ago.

"Do a little more of that, and gradually speed up a little. Let's see what happens."

Kathy began to ski a little faster. She was still walking her poles. Suddenly, as she set her edges, her skis whipped around in a quick parallel turn. She almost lost her balance, stood up, and then lost it again and fell. I skied up beside her and held out my hand to help her up.

She looked a little dazed. "What happened?" she asked me. "It felt like someone pulled the rug out from under me."

"I think you turned so fast that you couldn't handle it," I told her. "When you set your edges just right, your skis will start a turn. If you're not ready for it, it can lead to a fall. I think you've had enough for today. Go home and let all this sink in. Try it again in a few days."

"OK," she said, dusting the snow off her pants. "I'll see you later." I watched her ski cautiously down the hill.

I didn't see Kathy for about two weeks, and then I ran into her in the bar after skiing.

"Hey, guess what?" she said. "Your stuff works!"

"Tell me about it."

"Well," she said, "I stayed home for a day after we worked, and then I went back out again. I skied a little and then practiced those movements that you showed me, and then I would ski some more, and so on. After two days of that, it all came together somehow, and I began to use my poles just like you're supposed to, and to do parallel turns like there was nothing to it. The strangest thing is my arms. They almost seem to move in the way they're supposed to automatically." She looked down at her arms. "They still feel kind of weird.

"In fact, the whole turn feels strange. It doesn't feel anything like I had expected it to feel."

"That," I told her, "is the reason you couldn't do it in the first place."

Summary

Here's a summary of the movements I did with Kathy, to help her improve.

1. Stand at the side of the trail, with the uphill direction to your right, and plant your poles in the snow beside you. Keep your hands on the grips for balance. Bring your skis together, with the uphill ski leading, and bend your knees comfortably. Move your knees to the right and back several times, setting your uphill edges. Notice how far your knees move to the right. Repeat the movement of the knees and notice what you do with your upper body. What do you do with your hips, your spine, your ribs, and your head? Do these parts of the body assist in moving the knees to set the edges? (Fig 13–1)

Fig 13–1

2. Rest briefly, and then begin to move your left hip and shoulder closer together. In order to do this, you must bend your spine so that the left side of your body becomes shorter, and the right side becomes longer. As you make this movement, scan your body with your attention. Notice how your knees move to the right, how your hips tilt, your spine bends, and how the ribs are compressed on the left side and fan out on the right side. Let your left shoulder drop down and your right shoulder rise up as you bend your spine. Breathe easily as you move. (Fig 13–2)

3. Rest briefly, and then repeat the previous movement of bending the spine, bringing the left hip and shoulder closer together. As

Fig 13–2

you move, notice your neck and head. Do they assist in the movement of the spine? Continue moving and tilt your head to the left, so that your left ear approaches your left shoulder as you bend your spine. Notice how involving the head and neck in the movement allows the body to bend even more, so that the knees can move even further to the side. (Fig 13–3)

Fig 13–3

4. Rest briefly, and then repeat the previous movement a few more times, bending the whole body to the side and allowing the left ear to approach the left shoulder. Stop when you are bent as far to the side as you can go without strain. Holding your body still, tilt your head left and right about twenty times, so that the right ear approaches the right shoulder, and then the left ear approaches the left shoulder. If you don't stiffen your shoulders they will follow the head. (Fig 13–4A/B) Finally, repeat the movement of bending the whole body to the side, and notice how far

Fig 13–4A

Fig 13–4B

and how easily you can bend. How much further do your knees go to the side now that you have learned to involve your whole body in the edging movement?

5. Stop moving and rest. Close your eyes and compare the feeling in the left and right sides of your body. Which side feels bigger? Which side feels lighter? Which leg will support your weight better?

6. Turn around and try the exercise on the other side, with the uphill direction to your left. Now you will be bending your spine so that the right side of your body gets shorter and the left longer, while the knees move to the left.

7. Now try the bending movement while skiing very slowly back and forth across the trail. Begin with a small movement and gradually increase the amount of bending. As you move, scan your body with your attention. Feel how the pressure on the uphill sides of your feet increases as you bend to the side. Notice how your knees move to the side, how your spine bends, what your ribs do, how your shoulders move, and how one ear approaches the shoulder. After a few minutes, you should begin to get the feeling that your whole body is involved in the movement in a coordinated way. When the movement feels comfortable and easy, make a few turns on an easy trail. Can you make a turn by setting your edges?

14

Tom: The Myth of the Quiet Upper Body

Skiing, like other sports, has its share of myths. And one myth that causes skiers a lot of trouble is the idea of the "quiet upper body."

I ran head-on into this particular myth working with a man named Tom.

Tom had been skiing for about eight years and was an advanced skier. He could do a parallel turn under most conditions and could even ski the bumps fairly well, as long as the trail was not particularly steep and the bumps not too big.

Watching Tom ski down an intermediate hill, I admired his form. Plenty of skiers would give their right arm to ski that well.

I yelled at Tom to stop, and I skied up beside him. "Well," I said to him, "you look pretty good to me. What can I do for you?"

"You know," Tom replied, "most of my friends say that I ski well, and it's probably true. But on the inside, I feel kind of stiff. It's like I have to force my moves. It's not so much that I want to improve my form, but I want to use less force and effort." He looked at me. "Does that make sense?" he asked.

"It makes plenty of sense to me," I replied.

I had known other people like Tom. They were intelligent and hard-working, and usually successful at whatever they turned their hands to. A lot of them were successful businessmen.

However, many of these people had the habit of using a lot of force to accomplish their tasks. As a result, they usually attained their ends, but then they would have an internal feeling of unease that spoiled their pleasure.

In the world of business, this didn't matter so much, because being successful in business is usually equated with simply making money.

Skiing, however, is different. We ski for enjoyment, and an internal feeling of straining or forcing can spoil the experience, even if we have the accolades of envious friends to dampen the still, small voice inside that says, "You're missing something."

People like Tom usually like to jump right in and get to work, so I didn't waste any time.

I held out my hand. "Give me your poles," I said.

I took Tom's poles and set them on the snow. I had noticed that Tom's upper body seemed to be a little stiff when he was skiing, and I wanted to start working with the twisting movement of the body to loosen him up. The poles usually drag on the snow and get in the way in the beginning, so I ask the skier to put them down at first.

"Now," I directed Tom, "just turn your whole body left and right, and look to the left and right as you turn."

Tom began to turn with a hard, forceful movement to the left and right. He was holding his arms horizontal with his elbows bent so that his hands were close together near his chest. At each side, he exhaled explosively.

"What are you doing?" I asked him. "Trying to break your neck?"

"I'm stretching out my muscles," he replied. "That's what this exercise is for, isn't it?"

"Let me see if I understand you, Tom. Your idea is that if you practice using a lot of force in your movements, you will eventually wind up using less force? Is that right?"

Tom stopped turning. "I never thought of it like that," he said. "So how should I do it?"

"Let your arms drop," I said, "and turn gently to each side. Imagine that the movement is like a swing. You make an initial move to get the swing started, and then it only takes a very tiny push on each turn to keep it going. You kind of *let* yourself turn, instead of *making* yourself turn."

Tom began to turn left and right, letting his arms swing over to one side and then the other. As he turned, I began to direct his attention to different parts of his body.

"Notice what your feet are doing," I told him. "Now your ankles . . . your knees . . . hips . . ." Systematically, I directed Tom's attention to every part of his body. As he began to feel how his whole body was involved in the movement, the turning became easy and flowing, and nice to look at. Finally, after about five minutes of turning, Tom let out a big sigh and began to breathe easily.

"How does that feel?" I asked him.

"It feels good," he told me, "but what are we doing, if I'm not stretching my muscles?"

"If you stretch your muscles, you are just forcing them to get longer. That works in the short term, but in the long term you get stiffer, and have to use more and more force to get what you want. If you move easily and feel how each and every part of your body is involved in a movement, the muscles get longer spontaneously, and you reduce the amount of force you are using, instead of increasing it."

"OK," Tom said, "I'll buy that. What next?"

"I want you to try another simple movement, and then we are going to put the two movements together. Just bend your knees and hips, as if you were unweighting in a turn or going over a bump, and then straighten up."

Tom began to bob up and down, flexing and extending his hips, knees, and ankles. Again I directed his attention to scan through his body. Everything appeared to be going smoothly.

"OK," I said, "now let's put those two movements together and see what happens. Go back to the turning movement. As you turn to the left, flex your knees and hips, and as you turn to the right extend them, so that you start to squat down to the left, and then stand up to the right."

Tom began to turn as I watched. Right away I noticed something. As he started to add the bending movement of his body to the turning movement, he stiffened his neck and stopped turning his head.

"Keep turning, and pay attention to the distance between your chin and each shoulder. Tell me what you feel."

"Well," Tom said, "it stays the same. What does that mean?"

"It means that you stopped turning your head when you started to bend your knees. That stiffens your body a little. You probably do something like that when you're skiing.

"Go back to that movement, and make sure you don't stiffen your neck. Just think about moving your chin closer to one shoulder and then the other as you turn."

Tom resumed turning, this time more slowly, so that he could pay attention to his head movement. At first, because this was a new pattern of movement for him, he appeared to be a little stiff and hesitant. After a few minutes, however, the movement smoothed out. Then I asked him to begin to scan his body with his attention. As soon as he started thinking about his feet, he stopped turning his head. I pointed this out to him.

"Think about your feet, and then your head, then your knees, and then back to your head, and so on," I told him. "After you catch yourself stiffening your neck a few times, you'll stop doing it."

After several more minutes, Tom was turning and bending easily, and he had stopped stiffening his neck. I told him then to reverse the movement, so that he straightened his hips and knees as he turned to the left, and bent them as he turned to the right.

As soon as Tom reversed the movement, he again stiffened his neck. "Watch your neck," I said.

Tom grimaced as he started to turn his head. "Boy, that habit is really ingrained," he said.

After a few more minutes of turning to the right and bending down, and back to the left and standing up, I asked Tom to try two other patterns.

First I asked him to bend down as he turned to each side, and to stand up in the middle of the turn, when he was facing straight along his skis. Then I had him reverse that pattern, so that he was bent down in the middle of the turn, and standing up straight on each side. Towards the end of all this, I found that I rarely had to call his attention to his head and neck. They were moving freely all the time.

"Take a break, Tom, you've been working pretty hard," I said.

Tom stopped turning. "Yeah," he said. "The movements are pretty easy, but all that business of paying attention to the different parts of my body really gives my awareness a workout." He yawned and stretched. "Somehow, it's kind of relaxing, though," he added.

I reached over and retrieved Tom's poles, and handed them over to him. "Ready for stage two?" I asked.

"Let her rip," Tom replied, as he fixed his pole straps.

"I want you to do those same movements skiing slowly across the trail. Let's start with just the turning movement for a few times, and then we'll add the bending movements."

"You want me to ski while I'm twisting my body around like that?" he asked.

"Yeah," I said.

Tom gave me a funny look and began to ski across the trail, slowly twisting left and right. I followed close by and watched. Almost immediately, I got the feeling that something was wrong. Tom had a strained expression on his face, and his breathing was quick and shallow. He went about a hundred yards, and then came to an abrupt stop. He turned and looked at me. His face was hard. "This isn't right and I don't think I want to do it," he said with some force.

I was taken aback. "What isn't right?" I asked.

"When you ski, I know that you're supposed to keep a quiet upper body, not twist around all over the place like this."

"There's a big difference between a quiet upper body and a stiff upper body," I shot back.

Tom relaxed a little. "What do you mean?" he said.

"I mean that you have a stiff upper body, and that's what's messing up your skiing. I'm trying to get it loosened up."

"Wait a minute, I don't understand", Tom said. "I've heard for years that a good skier keeps a quiet upper body, and all the good skiers I see on the slope do that. Their upper body hardly moves at all. I've been working on keeping my upper body quiet for the last three seasons, and I don't want to spoil all that work."

"And how much have you improved in the last three seasons?" I asked Tom.

"Well, not that much, really," he replied. "But I still don't think it's right to throw my body around while I'm skiing. Nobody does that."

"Did you think I was asking you to *ski* like that?"

"Yeah, isn't that what I'm doing?"

"No, no," I said. "This whole procedure is an awareness exercise to get you to feel how you are stiffening your body when you ski, and to open up new patterns of movement for you to use when you're skiing. I'm not suggesting that you actually ski while twisting your body around like that."

"Well," said Tom, "Why didn't you say so?"

"I thought I did," I said.

"But what's the difference between a quiet upper body and a stiff upper body?" persisted Tom.

"Well," I replied, "to my way of thinking, the idea of a 'quiet upper body' is kind of a myth. I know that looking in from the outside it *looks* like the upper body is quiet, but in reality there is a lot going on there. For one thing, the muscles along the spine on each side have to be able to move to balance the shift of weight as the legs move from side to side to make the turn. And for that to happen, the neck has to be free.

"If your torso is stiff, like it is in a lot of people, it inhibits the ability of the body to balance and indirectly affects the ability of the legs to move easily.

"What we're doing with these movements is trying to give you the feeling that you can move your upper body *while you are skiing*. I know you can move your body while you're standing still.

"In fact, the inability to use what skiers call the upper body—the hips, spine, ribs, shoulders and neck—in an effective way is almost a universal problem with skiers. Very few skiers feel that in order to use the legs properly, they must do something with their hips, and that for the hips to move easily, the lower back must be free, and that for the lower back to move, the neck must not be held tight.

"In fact, that's just what you're doing when you ski: holding your neck tight. By moving slowly and with awareness, we were able to discover that. And once you can feel exactly how you are interfering with yourself, it's not so hard to let go."

"I see what you're driving at," said Tom. "Let's get back to work."

"Just continue like you were doing," I said. "I want you to repeat that series of movements you just did standing still, but this time while skiing slowly across the slope."

Tom began to ski across the slope. I followed and watched, occasionally telling him to pay attention to some part of his body, but mostly leaving him alone.

After making a few traverses while just turning his body left and right, he began to add the bending movement, as we had done earlier. He was onto the fact that he was stiffening his neck without knowing it, and now he corrected himself as soon as he felt his neck getting tight.

As I watched, the movements became easier and smoother, and Tom's breathing was easy and continuous, an almost certain sign that he was doing the movements without strain.

Finally he stopped and beckoned me to come over to him. "I feel like I've got it," he said. "What do we do now?"

"Make some turns," I told him. "Start out slowly, and think about your neck and your upper body, and just make sure that you don't stiffen them needlessly."

Tom started down the trail. It was a fairly easy intermediate-level trail with no bumps. It was hard for me to see a difference between the way Tom was skiing now and the way he had been skiing an hour before. He appeared to be skiing with a little less effort, but the difference was fairly subtle.

Tom skied a long way before he stopped. I skied up to him. "How is it?" I asked.

"I think it's working," he said. "That feeling of strain is just about gone. Also, I think I was holding my breath a lot before. Is that possible?"

"You probably were," I told Tom. "When you stiffen your neck, you almost always hold your breath. When you release your neck, the breathing tends to go on automatically, like it should."

"Great," Tom said. "What now?"

I felt that Tom had had plenty of instruction for now. He knew how to get what he wanted, and it was just a matter of time and practice.

"Just keep on doing what you were just doing," I said. "When your skiing feels easy, then you can go to a slightly more difficult slope. Just keep on increasing the difficulty, a little at a time. If you ever feel that you are stiffening yourself and that you can't let go, then back up to an easier slope for a while."

"Great," said Tom. "I'll catch you later." He turned and took off down the trail.

I didn't see or hear from Tom all the rest of that season, but in September I got a post card from him. All it said was, "Save an hour for me this winter."

Summary

Here is a summary of the movements I did with Tom to help him improve. As usual, pick a wide, flat, beginner or easy intermediate-level slope to do the movements.

1. Stand still at the side of the trail, and set your poles down beside you. Begin to turn your whole body left and right. As you turn, scan your body with your attention. Start at your feet and slowly think of your ankles, your knees, your hips, your spine, your ribs, your shoulders, your neck, your head, and finally your eyes. Look to each side as you turn, and let yourself breathe easily. Spend about five minutes slowly turning

like this, while scanning your body with your attention. (Fig 14–1A/B)

Fig 14–1A   Fig 14–1B

2. Now bend your knees, hips, and ankles until your knees are about at right angles, and then come back to your standing posture. Repeat this movement slowly and easily for two or three minutes while scanning your body with your attention. Be sure you let yourself breathe easily. (Fig 14–2A/B)

Fig 14–2A   Fig 14–2B

3. In this and the following exercises, we are going to combine the first two movements in several ways. By learning to have complete freedom to twist and bend your body in any combination of movements, you will improve your skiing.

Begin to turn your whole body left and right as you just did, but now, as you turn to the right, bend your knees so that you sink down, and as you turn to the left, straighten your knees so that you stand up. As you move, scan your body with your attention and notice if you stiffen any part of your body and inhibit the turning movement. Pay particular attention to your head and neck. Make sure you continue to turn your head so that your chin approaches each shoulder as you turn. (Fig 14–3A/B)

Fig 14–3A   Fig 14–3B

4. Turn your whole body left and right, but this time bend your knees as you turn to the left and straighten them to the right. (Fig 14–4A/B)

Fig 14–4A   Fig 14–4B

5. Turn your whole body left and right, and bend your knees as you turn to each side, and straighten them when you are facing the front. (Fig 14–5A/B)

Fig 14–5A   Fig 14–5B

6. Turn your whole body left and right, and bend your knees when you face straight to the front, and straighten them when you are turned to the side. (Fig 14–6A/B)

Fig 14–6A   Fig 14–6B

7. Pick up your poles and repeat the previous movements while skiing slowly across the trail. Start with a small movement and gradually increase the size of the movement as you feel more comfortable. When all of the movements feel fluid, make a few turns on an easy trail. How does your skiing feel?

15

Carol:
First Wind Up, Then Pitch

One way people get stuck in skiing is the result of a kind of narrowing of the attention. We reduce a problem to such a small area that we inadvertently exclude the solution.

In downhill skiing, like other human activities, no part is independent of the whole. All the parts of the body must cooperate in very precise ways to achieve the desired goal, which for a skier is a full parallel turn. Skiers often get stuck by thinking almost exclusively of their feet and legs, while virtually ignoring the activity of their upper body.

Also, to be assured of finding the solution, we must expand our awareness not only spatially, but also over time. The wind-up and the follow-through are just as important as the moment of action.

This kind of temporal narrowing of the attention turned out to be the problem for a woman named Carol.

Carol had been skiing for six years. She had applied herself diligently to her chosen sport, reading instructional manuals and taking lessons. As a result, she was very knowledgeable about skiing.

Carol moved well on skis. She didn't stiffen herself up like so many skiers do, and she appeared to be at ease when she skied, at least while traversing the slope.

However, she had "one big problem" that kept her from skiing well.

"When I start my turn," Carol told me, "it feels real awkward somehow. I feel as if I'm using a lot of force, and the movement is kind of jerky instead of being smooth and flowing, like I want it to be."

"Let's go have a look at your turn," I said. "I want to see exactly what you're talking about."

We left the warming hut where we had been talking and put on our skis. Carol started down the hill. She began on a long traverse. Appearing quite relaxed, she went almost all the way across the hill before she turned. As she had said, the start of her turn was stiff and awkward and appeared to be forced. The second part of the turn, though, after her skis had crossed the fall line, appeared easy and graceful.

I had to watch Carol make several turns before I could see what her difficulty was.

I skied down and caught up with her. "Hold up," I said. "I've seen enough."

"What do you think?" Carol asked.

"I know how to get you moving like you want," I told her. "Are you ready to go?"

"Let's do it," she said, starting to turn her skis down the hill.

"Hold it a second. I want to show you something before we jump into the skiing."

Carol turned her skis back and stood up. "I'm all ears," she said.

"I want you to try something. Just jump up in the air a few inches."

"Just jump up, that's all?" Carol asked.

"That's all," I replied.

Carol crouched down and then jumped up, lifting her skis a few inches off the snow. "Again?" she asked.

"Yeah, do it a couple or three times, and just notice what you do to jump," I said.

Carol jumped up several times. There was nothing remarkable about the jump. She went up and came down easily, like anybody would.

"That seems easy enough," she said. "What's the point?"

"We're getting to that," I said. "But first, I want you to try to jump up without bending your knees first. Try that and find out what happens."

"That's impossible," said Carol.

"I know, but try it anyway. I want you to feel something."

Dutifully, Carol tried to jump without bending her knees first. She held her breath and threw her arms around in an awkward way. In spite of expending a lot of effort, she hardly moved at all.

Carol relaxed and looked at me. "How does that feel?" I asked her.

"Really stiff and awkward," she replied.

"Does that remind you of anything you do when you're skiing?"

Carol hesitated before replying. "Not really," she said. "Should it?"

"I mean the feeling of awkwardness, not just the movement itself. Think about it for a minute. Imagine that you're going to do a turn. Just go through it mentally."

Carol closed her eyes. After a minute she opened them and looked at me.

"You know, that's kind of the same feeling that I get when I try to start my parallel turn. I get kind of tense, and I feel like I'm fighting myself somehow. Should I bend my knees before I turn?"

"It's not quite that simple," I said, "but you're definitely on the right track.

"Your problem is not what you do as you turn, Carol. It's what you do, or actually what you don't do, just *before* you turn. Like trying to jump without bending your knees first. So now we're going to make it happen. Ready?"

"Yep," Carol said. "Let's go."

"OK. Bend your knees and hips as if you were skiing. Bend your elbows too. Good. Now, do you remember that old dance called The Twist?" Carol nodded. "Just do that movement standing there a few times." Carol began to twist her hips and shoulders in opposite directions.

"Just keep doing that, and let yourself breathe easily, and began to scan your body with your attention, so you can feel how each part moves. Start by feeling your ankles, then your knees, then hips, shoulders, and all the way up to your head."

I watched as Carol did The Twist. As she directed her attention to each part of her body, the movement became smoother and easier. I let her have as much time as she needed to become comfortable with the motion.

"Stop moving and tell me what you do to make that movement," I said.

Carol said, "Well, I rotate my hips left and right, and my arms and shoulders in the opposite direction. That's right, isn't it?"

"Exactly," I replied. "Now, just do that same thing while you're skiing very slowly across the hill."

Carol began to ski on a long traverse, twisting her hips and shoulders in opposite directions. I stayed close behind her and directed her to feel what each part of her body did as she moved. At first she was a little awkward, because she wasn't used to moving her body in that particular way while sliding across the snow. But in a few minutes, as she began to feel how her whole body was involved in the motion, she began to do it easily.

After about ten minutes I began to see what I had been looking for. The movement of Carol's upper body started to go down to her skis, so that they turned a little left and right as she twisted her hips and shoulders.

I caught up with Carol. "Notice what your skis are doing as you move your hips and shoulders," I said.

"They're turning a little bit left and right," she said. "Is that what you mean?"

"Yeah, that's what I mean. Now, I want you to exaggerate one part of that movement."

Carol had stopped on a traverse with her right side downhill. "Keep going across the hill, like you were just doing," I said, "and when you move your right hip forward and your right shoulder back, make it a quick, snapping movement. It helps to think about pulling your right elbow backward as you do that. Just try it and find out what happens."

153

Carol began to move across the hill. The first few times she tried the movement, she stiffened her legs, and her skis did not respond to the movement of her hips and shoulders. After ten or so trys, however, she started to become more comfortable with the motion, and as she rotated her shoulders to the right by moving her right elbow and shoulder backward, and her right hip forward, her skis turned sharply to the left, and she came to an abrupt stop.

"What happened?" I asked Carol.

"My skis just suddenly turned to the side, and I stopped," she replied.

"Did your skis turn, or did you turn them?"

"Well, I must have done it, but I've never turned them like that before."

"Do that a few more times," I directed, "so that you can feel exactly what you're doing with your upper body to turn the skis."

Carol started out again, rotating her hips and shoulders, and feeling how her skis turned a little to point uphill, and so arrested her progress. Soon, she was at the side of the trail.

"Turn yourself around, and try it going back the other way, with your left side downhill. This time, you'll pull your left elbow and shoulder backward, and your left hip will go forward. It's the same movement, but on the other side."

Again I watched as Carol moved slowly across the hill. This time it only took her three trys to get the movement of her upper body to transfer itself down to her skis. I followed her back and forth across the slope for about twenty minutes, letting her become familiar with the movement. Occasionally I would notice that some part of Carol's body was stiff, and I would direct her attention there, so she could feel the tension and let it go.

Finally she stopped. "This is starting to feel nice," she said. "I wonder why I never felt this movement before. Do you know?"

"I don't really know myself," I told Carol. "All I really understand is how to get people to improve. Exactly why they are stuck is a different question, and usually tough to answer.

"By the way, did you notice that when you got the movement just right, your skis stayed together as they turned? They were separating a little bit before."

Carol looked down at her skis. "Now that you mention it, I did. They just seemed to stay together automatically. I didn't have to do anything to make them stay together. Why is that?"

"When your weight is balanced just right, your skis will stay together without effort," I told her. "It's the most efficient way. But I want you to notice something else. When you rotate your hips and shoulders in opposite directions and turn your skis uphill and stop, do you feel that you bend your knees a little?"

Carol looked up, as if trying to remember her previous movements. "I think I did—I can't really remember for sure," she said.

"Try it again and find out," I said.

Carol began to ski slowly across the hill, pulling her downhill elbow and shoulder backward. As her skis turned slightly uphill, she would bend her knees. She made about ten movements and then stopped.

"I feel it," she said. "I do bend my knees a little. Why is that?"

"It's the natural thing to do," I replied. "When you turn your skis to the side and stop, the pressure on the soles of your feet increases, and the tendency is to bend your knees slightly to absorb the force. Try it again, and exaggerate the knee bending. I want you to feel something."

Carol started to ski across the hill again, rotating her hips and shoulders to turn her skis uphill and stop. As her skis turned, she would bend her knees, just as I asked. Every other traverse, I asked her to bend her knees even more.

Finally, I asked Carol to stop. "Now I want you to try something I call 'the controlled fall,'" I said. "Do just what you were doing, but this time bend your knees all the way, so that your rear end touches the back of your boots, and then fall into the hill, towards the uphill direction. You only have to fall a few inches, so it won't hurt."

Carol started to ski across the slope with the downhill direction to her right. She pulled her right elbow backward, rotating her skis to the left, and simultaneously bent her knees. As she stopped, she fell to the left.

"Did you bend your knees all the way?" I asked.

"Yeah, I think so," she replied.

"Look at the distance between your rear and the heels of your boots," I said.

Carol craned her neck around to the right and looked down. There was a gap of about eight inches between her behind and her heels.

"That's funny," she said. "I thought I bent my knees all the way, but I didn't."

"Yeah," I told her. "Just about everybody does that the first few times. When we are learning to ski, we spend so much time fighting to stay up that we forget how to bend our knees all the way. Do some more of those," I said, reaching out my hand to help her up, "and really bend your knees. The idea is to feel how much freedom you have to bend them, and then you won't stiffen them without knowing it."

After another twenty minutes, Carol could do the 'controlled fall' easily, and her rear was almost touching her boots as she tipped over onto the snow. We were back at the bottom of the hill, so we skied over and got on the lift.

"Whew," Carol said, "my mind feels like it's been through a wringer. Those are some strange movements. But tell me something. We started out with that jumping movement, and then you took me into all those other strange motions. What's the connection?"

"Well," I said, "to jump, you first have to bend your knees, right?"

Carol nodded. "In other words, if you want to go up, first you have to go down. And if you want to throw a ball forward, you first have to move it backward, like a pitcher's wind-up."

"So," I continued, "if you want to turn your skis downhill to make a parallel turn, the initial movement is to turn the skis uphill. That's the 'wind-up' for the parallel turn.

"And one of the things that makes downhill skiing such an exhilarating sport is the fact that the end of one turn is the 'wind-up' for the next turn, so a good skier just makes an effortless series of continuous oscillating movements. Most skiers call that linked parallel turns. You're always turning, so there's no traverse between the turns."

"I think I see what you're driving at," Carol said. "I can't wait to do that."

"Probably won't be too long now," I said.

The lift arrived at the top, and we got off. I picked a wide, flat, intermediate slope. "Try that same movement a few more times," I told Carol. "Just pull your downhill elbow back, and let your downhill hip move forward, so that your skis turn uphill a little, but this time don't stop, just slow down a little. Bend your knees as you do that, and then think about letting your skis turn back the other way, so that the tips point downhill."

Carol started out and I watched. She began by really snapping her downhill elbow backward, and I could see that she was stiffening up a little. I skied up behind her. "Give yourself a little slack," I said. "Rome wasn't built in a day."

"OK," she said, taking a deep breath and rolling her shoulders around.

I watched as Carol began to traverse the hill, moving her hips and shoulders and bending her knees to turn her skis. I could see that she was experimenting with the components of the movements, going a little faster, then a little slower, bending her knees a little more, then a little less, and so on.

After about five minutes, she hit on the right combination, and her body fell into the turn. I watched as she made about a dozen perfect linked parallel turns. Involuntarily, I held my breath. Suddenly Carol stiffened up and fell. Both bindings released, and her skis, poles, goggles and hat flew off in six different directions. I covered my eyes with my hand. I hate to see skiers fall like that. It brings back too many personal memories. I uncovered my eyes. "Yard sale!" someone yelled from the nearby chair.

"Hey, everybody looks good on the lift," I yelled back, as I skied over to Carol.

She was sitting up in the snow, her eyes as wide as saucers. "Is that *it?*" she said. "Wow!"

She started to scramble around for her equipment. "Take it easy, take it easy," I said. I wanted to spare Carol the experience that I had years ago of not being able to get back into my "perfect turn."

Carol collected her gear and got ready to ski again. I didn't think she had heard me. She started to point her skis down the hill. I reached over and grabbed her collar from behind. "Just hang on a second, will you?"

She took a deep breath and looked back at me. "What is it?" she asked impatiently.

"Just humor me and try the exercise a few more times. It'll work better that way, I promise you."

Carol relaxed a little. "OK, OK," she said. "I guess I was getting a little ahead of myself."

She went back to the exercise, and this time it took less than a minute for her to hit on the exact combination of movements that started the linked parallel turns. I watched as she made about ten turns and stopped. I skied up to where she was standing and came to a halt just beside her.

"That is absolutely the most unbelievable thing I have ever experienced, and it's so easy! Listen," she said, looking me right in the eye, "I'd like to stay around, but I don't want to quit."

So saying, she took off down the hill, still doing what appeared to be perfect linked parallel turns. I followed her all the way to the bottom. As near as I could see, she didn't miss a single turn.

Summary

Here's a summary of the movements I did with Carol to help her improve.

1. Find a wide, flat, beginner or easy intermediate-level trail. Stand at the side of the trail and set your poles down beside you. Bend your knees and elbows, as if you were in your skiing

stance. Begin to rotate your hips and shoulders in opposite directions, just like in the old dance called The Twist. Spend several minutes at this movement, all the while scanning your body with your attention. Make sure that all the parts move easily. Try the twisting movement with your weight a little towards your toes, then towards your heels, then towards the left, then the right, to get the feeling that you can do it with your weight in any position. (Fig 15–1A/B)

Fig 15–1A

Fig 15–1B

2. Pick up your poles and begin to ski slowly across the trail, still rotating your hips and shoulders in opposite directions. When you reach the opposite side of the trail, stop, turn around, and come back on the opposite traverse. As the movement becomes easy, you will notice that your skis turn a little left and right. Continue to move, and exaggerate the part of the movement where the tips of the skis

Fig 15–2

turn uphill a little. To do this, pull your downhill elbow backward with a quick, snapping movement. As the skis turn uphill,
bend your knees a little. When you can let the skis turn easily,
you will find that you come to a stop as you do this movement. (Fig 15–2)

3. Continue the previous movement and begin to speed up, so
that you are moving faster across the slope just before you turn
your skis and stop. Each time you stop, bend your knees as
much as you can. At the instant you come to a complete stop,
fall sideways into the hill, so that your buttocks touch the snow
just uphill of the skis. Look around and notice the distance
between your rear end and
the heels of your boots.
Continue the exercise until
you can bend your knees as
far as they will go, so that
your buttocks come very
close to or actually touch
your heels just as you fall.
(Fig 15–3)

Fig 15–3

4. Repeat the movement of
Exercise 3 a few more times,
moving your hips and shoulders to turn the tips of the skis
uphill and stop. Bend your knees as much as you need to feel
comfortable, but don't fall. Scan your body as you do the stopping movement. What do your toes do? Your knees? Your hips
and shoulders? Do your hold your breath? When the movement feels easy, continue; but now don't stop, just slow down
a little, then turn your ski tips back toward the fall line. Pay
attention to what you do with the rest of your body as you do
this. When you succeed, you will find that your tips continue to
turn downhill, across the fall line, and then come up on the
other traverse. In other words, you have made a parallel turn.

16

Ed: The Three Primary Movements Of Skiing

Ed was a long-time friend of mine whom I had worked with for several years. He would get a lesson from me whenever he felt the urge, and over time he had progressed from a beginner to a solid advanced level.

I went over to Ed's place one evening. He had a copy of one of the national ski magazines open to a picture of one of the current Olympic hopefuls rounding a slalom pole at warp speed. It was a good action shot. Looking at it, you could almost feel the excitement of the race and hear the skis carve through the snow.

"Man, I wish I knew how those guys do that," Ed said to me. "That kind of skiing is on another whole level from what us peons do."

"Well," I said to Ed, "those racers don't have any extra joints or a different set of muscles than you and I do, so what's the difference?"

"I don't know. Maybe it's divine guidance. What do you think?"

"Look at that picture," I told Ed. "What do you see?"

"I see a guy going around a pole at least twice as fast as I ever will," he said.

"Yeah, but look at the position of his body. What's he doing there?"

"Well, he's crouched down and kind of twisted around, I guess. Is that what you mean?"

"Yeah, sort of, but you could be a lot more specific," I told Ed. "Have you figured out the plan or the design of the way I taught you to ski?"

"Well, I don't guess so," said Ed. "All I remember is that my skiing kept getting easier and better. Most of the time I couldn't figure out what you were doing with me, but somehow I always improved."

"There's a method to what I do," I told Ed. "Think back to the beginning, when we first started working. Do you remember what we did?"

"At first we did a whole lot of things with the soles of my feet. I remember thinking that my feet were going to college and getting a Ph.D. That was a real education. Then later the lessons seemed to involve the rest of the body. Is that what you mean?"

"That's what I'm talking about, but there's a lot more. I'll tell you about it, and I think it'll help you to understand that picture in a different way.

"The first few lessons we did were all based on feeling how the pressure shifts on the bottoms of your feet as you lean forward and back, and as you tilt your skis left and right, and as you shift your weight left and right, and so on. That kind of awareness is crucial to high-level skiing, and very few people have it. It's not that they can't feel the soles of their feet, of course, it's just that they don't feel the functional connections between how the pressure is distributed on the soles of the feet and what is going on in their skis and body.

"After that, we did four different kinds of lessons. Do you know what they were?"

Ed shook his head. "I'm lost. Tell me what we did."

"We worked, one at a time, with what I call the three primary movements of skiing, and then we combined those three movements in several different ways."

I peered at Ed with a questioning look. He shrugged and turned his hands palms up, and looked off to one side.

"The first movement is twisting the body left and right about a vertical axis; the second is bending and straightening the ankles, knees, and hips; and the third is bending the body to the side. With each one of those three movements we did a number of variations and combinations."

Ed peered off into space for a minute. Finally he said, "I think I see what you're talking about. I do remember thinking there was some kind of organization in what you were doing with me, but I couldn't figure out exactly what it was."

"Well, that's it. We worked with each one of those three movements until they were clear in your awareness, and then we worked with some combinations of the movements. You can make just about any movement you need to on skis by combining those three movements in different ways. After a certain amount of work, your Moving Mind performed some kind of reorganization and you could ski a whole lot better."

"Yeah," Ed said, with a wistful look in his eyes. "I remember that one big breakthrough about a year ago. I thought I had died and gone to heaven. I still don't understand how something like that is possible. I never dreamed I could ski like that. How do you explain that, anyway? I know you're always talking about the 'Moving Mind,' but that's just a name."

"Well," I said, "you're right about that. But if we don't have names, we can't talk. As long as you don't get lost in the words, though, you can learn.

"But here's my 'explanation.' After working with a lot of people and teaching them to ski at a much higher level, I realized that the real work of learning to ski is performed by a different part of the mind from the part that thinks in words and reasons logically. I have two different ways of thinking about what happens when you have one of those 'breakthroughs.'

"The first way is like this. When you have a breakthrough, you have the subjective sensation that you're suddenly skiing perfectly, and someone watching from the outside can see it. That makes me think there is a part of the mind that somehow knows how to do that, and ordinarily we interfere with that part and somehow stop it from doing what it needs to do. If the interference can be turned off, then the other part—which I call the Moving Mind—is free to do its job, and it just does it. So a lot of the teaching is about getting rid of the interference. It's an unlearning or a not-doing as opposed to a learning or a doing."

"What about the other way?" Ed asked.

"The other way is like this," I said. "In our society we place a lot of emphasis on thinking and reasoning and understanding. If you look at our educational process in 20th-century Western society, that's practically the whole thing. Memorizing huge amounts of words and figures, and then giving them back on a test.

"In our formative years, most of us learn to act from an intellectual, thinking, reasoning viewpoint. We learn to cover up and hide that part of the mind that deals with movement and spontaneity. So, the other way of looking at what happens when you have a breakthrough is to say that control of the body is transferred from the intellectual part of the mind, the part that thinks in words, to the Moving Mind."

"So which way is right?" Ed asked.

"There's probably some truth in each way, and neither is completely correct," I told him.

"But what about the emotional part? How do you explain that? I remember feeling I had finally found my place in the universe for a week after I had that big breakthrough."

"That's even harder to explain, but here's how I think of it. In our Western, analytical thinking, we usually divide our being up into pieces. We talk about 'mental' work, 'physical' work, 'emotional' work, and even 'spiritual' work, as if they were different things entirely. In reality, we are one whole being, and every part affects every other part.

"To put it in more concrete terms, if you want to 'find your place in the universe,' you have to have a certain posture, and a certain breathing, and a certain kind of thinking."

"Hey, you know," Ed said, "I had almost forgotten about it, but I remember that for a week after the breakthrough, all the time I was feeling high, my breathing felt real open and easy. Later on it closed down, and I didn't feel the same. Is that what you mean?"

"That's it exactly. When you learn to sustain that kind of breathing and posture, you can sustain the mental state."

"I sure would like to get back to that," Ed said. "It was the ultimate."

"I know what you mean," I told him. "Why do you think I ski every time I get the chance? It's not just for the fresh air and exercise.

"What throws people off when they go searching for that kind of feeling, I think, is that they rarely think about something as mundane as their body: their muscles, their posture, their breathing, and so on.

"But here's an interesting fact: the entire nervous output of the brain, 100% of what comes out of our thinking machine, is nerve impulses directed to the muscles. Therefore, you can deduce that almost everything that goes on in the brain has to do with movement. If the movement function remains static, it's virtually impossible to make a fundamental change in your thinking or emotions."

"So what pulls us back down to earth?" Ed asked.

"Old habits, I guess."

"Then how do we get back up there?"

"Keep skiing."

"How did you figure out all these weird exercises, anyway?" Ed asked me.

"Some years ago I was lucky enough to meet a man named Moshe Feldenkrais, who understood learning in a way that no one, as far as I know, has ever understood before. I studied with him for a few years, and then I applied his ideas to skiing, and I had one of those big breakthroughs, and here I am.

"A lot of people thought of Feldenkrais as some kind of healer. He could do amazing things with stroke victims, and people who had been in accidents, or had whiplash injuries, or other problems.

"But the real essence of his work goes far beyond that. It's difficult to put in words exactly what he did, but you can experience it when you ski, if you go about it in the right way."

"Suppose you had to condense all of these ideas into just a few words. Sort of the essence of it all. Could you do that?" Ed asked.

"I can do it, but I don't know how much good it will do. The essential idea is really pretty simple: you must use your whole body in the most efficient way in every move you make.

So the question to ask yourself, if you have a certain move that you want to do on skis, is, 'To make this movement, what must I do with my whole body?'

"So, for example, if you want to edge your skis, you find that you move your knees to one side, and then one hip has to be higher, and so the spine must bend, and the ribs must get shorter on one side, the shoulders must do something, and the neck should go along with the rest of the spine.

"And when you get down into the real details, you find that for your neck to be free, you have to do something with your jaw, and your eyes, and your breathing.

"So all the lessons I give are really about expanding awareness. That is, about involving more of yourself in a movement. I almost never actually tell someone how to make a particular move, such as a parallel turn. If they can't do it, my explaining it won't really help them to improve. However, once they have a certain level of awareness, they will find that the move comes spontaneously, almost like magic."

Ed looked down at the table. "Hey. I had almost forgotten about this photo and the three primary movements of skiing. What were you going to show me?"

"Have you still got your Polaroid camera?" I asked him.

"Yeah—do you want me to get it out?"

"Yeah," I told him.

Ed got his camera and gave it me. "All ready to go," he said.

"OK. Here's what I want you to do. Stand about a foot away from this wall, with your right side toward the wall, and point your toes a little in toward the wall.

"Now, what I want you to do is to make the three primary movements of skiing, all at the same time, and do almost the maximum amount of each movement. That means that you bend your knees, hips and ankles, you turn to the left, and you bend to the side, so that you shorten the left side of your body. Lean your right shoulder against the wall for support."

Ed crouched down as I had said, leaning against the wall.

"Good," I said. "Now, move your left foot away from your right a little, and hold both hands out in front as if you had ski poles in your hands."

I got out in front of Ed and snapped a picture with the camera. "Come over here and look at this," I told him.

I set the photo down next to the picture of the racer in the ski magazine. It was still developing.

Ed watched intently as the photo developed.

"It's almost exactly the same," he said. "I'm in the same position as the racer."

"That's right," I told him. "The racers push themselves to the maximum. I asked you to flex, turn, and bend almost as far as you could, and that put you into that 'racer's position.'"

"So is that all there is to it? If I want to ski like that I just do what you showed me?"

"Well, you were standing still, and leaning against a wall, and the racer is sliding around a pole at thirty or forty miles an hour. Plus, you have to develop a lot of strength in your legs to hold yourself up when you turn that sharply. But in essence, I think that's it."

"I don't know," Ed said. "Maybe I'll give it a try."

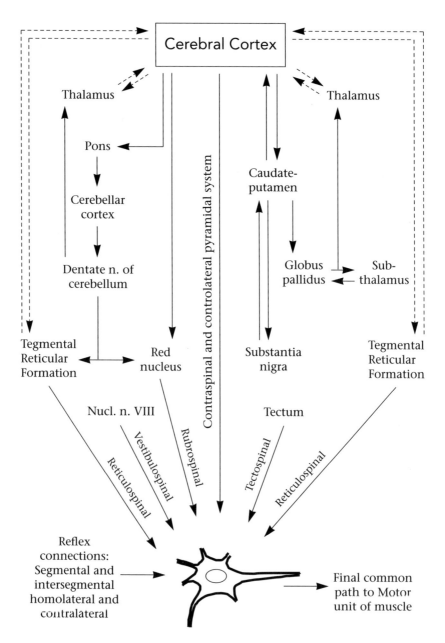

Figure A–1. Descending Nerve Tracts Affecting The Final Common Path (Adapted from *Languages of the Brain*, by Karl H. Pribram. Used by permission.)

APPENDIX

The Neurophysiology of the Moving Mind

(This appendix is presented for those who are interested in the neurophysiological details of the Moving Mind.)

The idea that there is a Moving Mind, a semi-autonomous part of the brain that controls most of our movements, is based on the fact that the majority of the nerve impulses arriving at the final common path originate in the evolutionarily old part of the brain. The structures in this part of the brain are considered to act automatically, more or less independent of the conscious, voluntary will.

Anatomically, the Moving Mind consists of the sub-cortical structures shown in Figure A–1—that is, everything except for the cerebral cortex.

In this schematic anatomical illustration, it is possible to see clearly how the majority of the nerve impulses reaching the muscles originate in the lower centers of the brain, which I have called the Moving Mind. However, when we are moving, we usually have no real sense of what part of our brain is directing the movement. It is easier to get a feeling of how our brain directs our body to move by thinking functionally. From a functional standpoint then, the Moving Mind consists of the following structures (Fig A–2):

1. *The postural mechanisms.* In experiments done in the early part of this century, it was shown conclusively that the postural mechanisms in the higher animals and to some extent in men are automatic. There is a special system of nerves and muscle fibers (the red or "slow twitch" fibers) that are responsible for

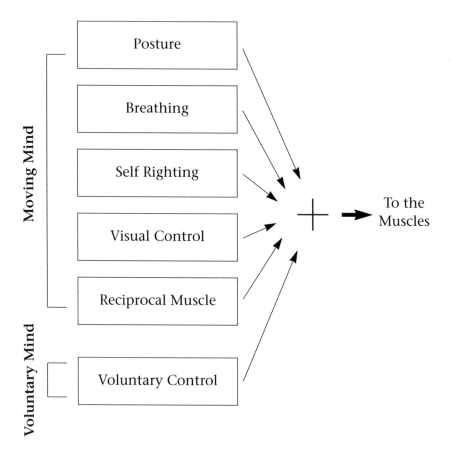

Figure A–2. The Moving Mind from a functional standpoint.

posture. These muscles are able to contract and remain contracted without fatigue for long periods of time. When the postural mechanisms are allowed to function without interference, one may have the feeling of being held up by an outside agent.

Usually, if posture is not what it should be, it means that somehow the automatic postural mechanisms are being interfered with. To improve posture, therefore, we must find the interference and let go of it.

2. *The self-righting mechanisms.* While the postural mechanisms are relatively static, the self righting mechanisms are more dynamic. Their operation is most noticeable whenever we get off balance and are about to fall. Just about everyone has had the experience of slipping on a patch of ice or some other slippery surface, and feeling how the arms and legs move quickly and automatically to try to keep the body from falling. These self-righting mechanisms are in operation all the time, although we are not usually aware of them unless we get into a critical balance situation. As you might expect, in skiing, you are in a permanent situation of critical balance, and the self righting mechanisms are of overriding importance for proper movement.

3. *The visual control mechanisms.* In the higher animals and especially in human beings, there are many automatic paths involving the eyes that direct movement. Most of these mechanisms are also outside of conscious control or awareness.

   This is the reason why some people are able to hit and catch a ball with ease, while others always seem to find themselves hitting thin air, or in the wrong position when the pop fly comes down, no matter how much they practice hitting and catching.

   In skiing, these visual control mechanisms are of great importance, especially when skiing a slope with many sudden terrain changes, like a mogul field. The body must be able to react to visual cues instantly to deal with the ups and downs of the slope.

4. *The reciprocal muscle relationship.* Every muscle in the body has another muscle or group of muscles that acts in opposition to it. For example, the biceps muscle, in the front of the upper arm, acts to bend the elbow. The triceps muscle, in the back of the arm, acts in the opposite way to straighten the elbow. (Physiologists call this the agonist-antagonist relationship.) The nervous mechanisms that control this function are mostly in the spine, and again, they operate automatically. Therefore, when we make a movement such as bending our elbow, we just "bend the elbow," and the automatic mechanisms con-

trol the lengthening of one muscle and the shortening of the other.

In the center of the body, with the muscles of the torso, this relationship is extremely complex. For example, if we bend forward, rounding the spine in back, the muscles in the front of the body become shorter, and the muscles in the back must become longer. If, on the other hand, we bend the spine to one side, so that the muscles on the right side of the spine get shorter, then the muscles on the left side of the spine must get longer. In the second case, muscles that worked in opposition to each other in the first case (one contracting while the other decontracts) now work along with each other (both muscles contracting and decontracting together). If we think about twisting the spine, turning the head to the left and the hips to the right, we can imagine yet a different relationship of these muscles.

It is fortunate that all this works automatically. If we had to think about all these details of the muscle movements, it would take us all day just to get out of bed, and fast, coordinated movements like those involved in skiing would be impossible.

5. *Breathing.* Proper breathing movements using the diaphragm, the big breathing muscle that divides the chest from the abdomen, are activated by involuntary structures in the nervous system that monitor the carbon dioxide level of the blood, and initiate an inhalation when the body requires more oxygen. Usually, if the breathing function is not well organized, it is because of some interference with the breathing muscles. Those who do not breathe well are usually stiffening their chest and spine without knowing it. It is, of course, possible to control breathing voluntarily, but this voluntary breathing uses a different set of muscles from the involuntary breathing that involves the diaphragm.

For this reason, "deep breathing" exercises, which exercise the voluntary breathing muscles, rarely produce any lasting beneficial results, and sometimes they actually cause damage, by promoting strain in the breathing apparatus.

Fortunately, this interference can be removed, and then the breathing will improve spontaneously.

From the above analysis it can be seen that the idea that we can voluntarily control all our movements is a myth, a myth that has been causing those who want to learn to improve performance a tremendous number of problems. Once the idea of reprogramming the Moving Mind is grasped, however, large improvements may be made very quickly.

In the sport of downhill skiing, the operation of the Moving Mind is particularly conspicuous. The Moving Mind comes into operation in the most obvious way when we move quickly, or, when balance is a critical issue. Therefore, in the middle of a parallel turn at high speed, the Moving Mind is running the body. This makes downhill skiing the perfect sport to reorganize the Moving Mind so that it functions at a much higher level. When this is done, all the functions of life improve.

Books about the Feldenkrais Method

Books by Moshe Feldenkrais

Body and Mature Behavior: A Study of Anxiety, Sex, Gravitation and Learning. NY: International Universities Press, 1949.

Awareness Through Movement: Health Exercises for Personal Growth. NY: Harper and Row, 1972.

The Case of Nora: Body Awareness as Healing Therapy. NY: Harper and Row, 1977.

The Elusive Obvious, or, Basic Feldenkrais. Cupertino, CA: Meta Publications, 1981.

The Master Moves. Cupertino, CA: Meta Publications, 1984.

The Potent Self: A Guide to Spontaneity. NY: Harper and Row, 1985.

Books by Other Authors

Mindful Spontaneity. By Ruthy Alon. (Prism Press) NY: Avery Publishing, 1990.

Running With The Whole Body. By Jack Heggie. Emmaus, PA: Rodale Press, 1986.

The Feldenkrais Method: Teaching by Handling. By Yochanan Rywerant. NY: Giniger—Harper and Row, 1983.

Relaxercise. By David and Kaethe Zemach-Bersin, and Mark Reese. NY: Harper and Row, 1990.

About the Author

Jack Heggie earned a Bachelor of Science degree in physics from the Colorado School of Mines and worked as a digital computer engineer for ten years before studying with Moshe Feldenkrais, D.Sc. and becoming a practitioner of the Feldenkrais Method.®

Heggie is noted for his innovative practical applications of Feldenkrais' method of movement learning. He has designed special programs for runners, musicians, and skiers, and has written about the Feldenkrais approach for *Skiing, Northwest Skier, Boston SportScape, Snow Country*, and *Somatics* magazines. Heggie is also the author of *Running With The Whole Body*, a book that applies the Feldenkrais Awareness Through Movement® principles to running.

Heggie has been skiing for thirty years. He lives in Boulder, Colorado, where he maintains a private practice in the Feldenkrais Method of Functional Integration.®